I0488368

Botanical Illustration in Gouache

The Four Seasons

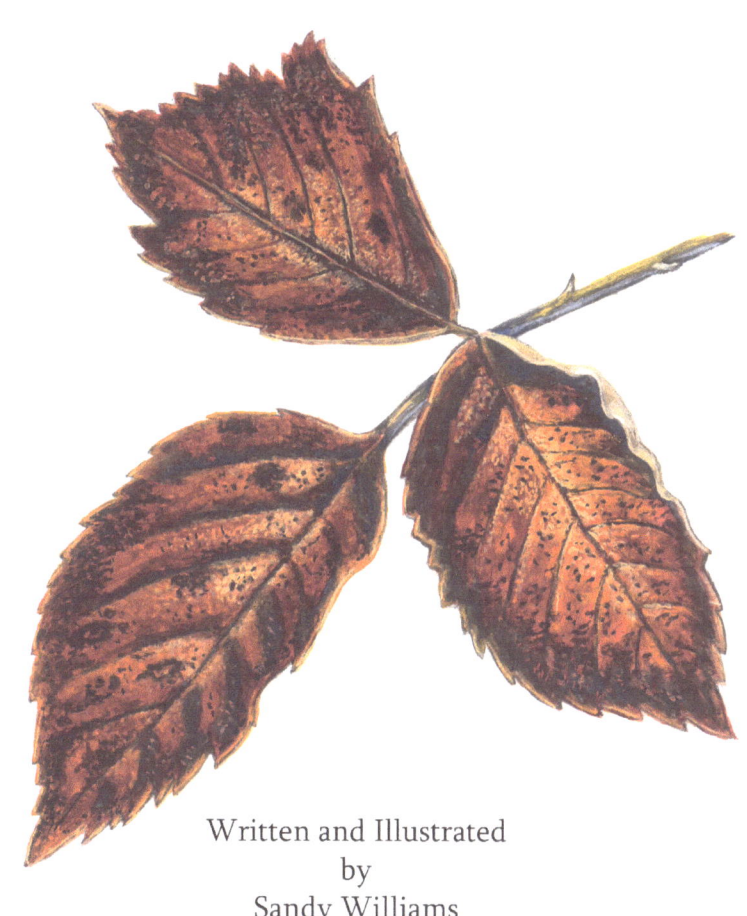

Written and Illustrated
by
Sandy Williams

Index

Botanical Illustration in Gouache
The Four Seasons

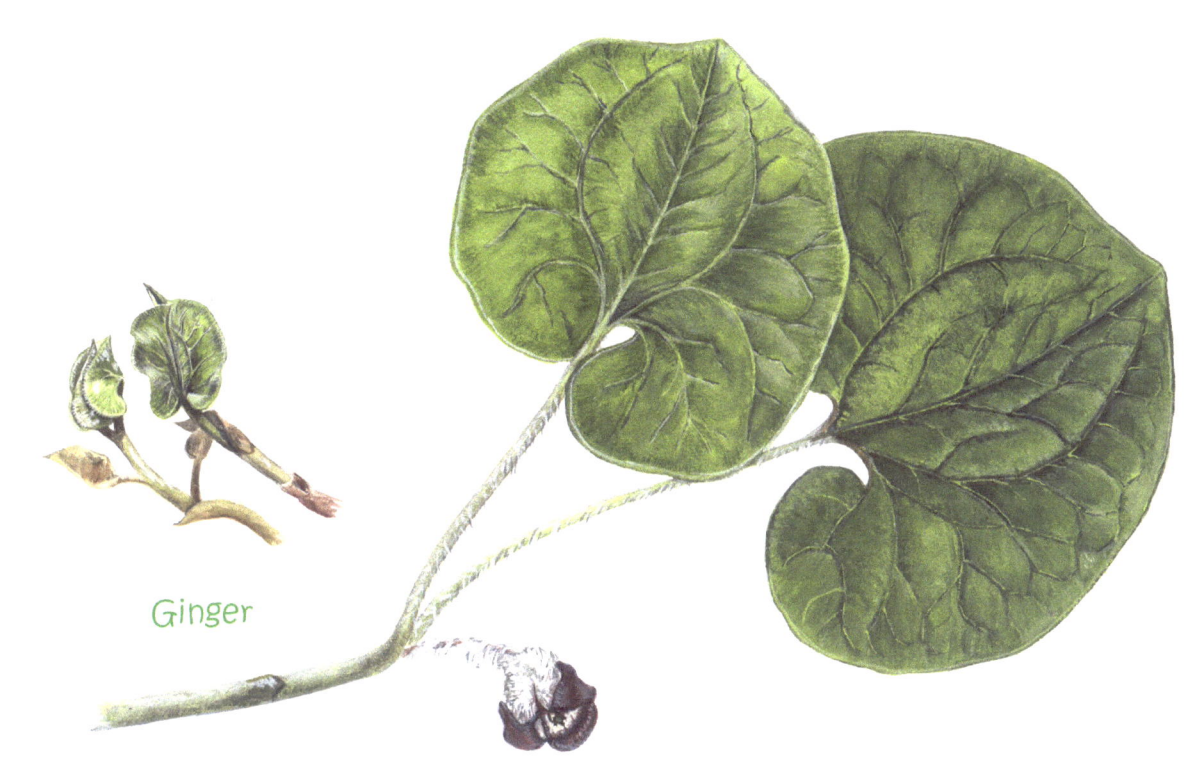

Ginger

Introduction

During the 1930's gouache was frequently used in advertising because of the even tones and bright colors it could produce. Its roots in beautifully illuminated manuscripts in the early evolution of the printed page were forgotten and it was no longer considered to be a medium for "serious" art. In the past few years gouache has enjoyed a resurgence in popularity for many reasons.

Gouache doesn't have the chemical fumes associated with oil paint. It dries quickly but can be reworked, even years later, unlike acrylics which dry quickly and then can't be changed. Gouache is economical because the paint can be reconstituted after it dries on the pallette by merely adding water. But, most of all, gouache is the perfect medium to paint extremely fine details, with either bright or subtle colors, and has a beautiful, suede like finish. Its my favorite medium to paint my wildlife and botanical work and, in this book, I hope to show you, in step by step demonstrations, the techniques used when painting seasonal botanicals. The purpose of this book is to guide you along so you can use these techniques when creating your own botanical illustrations.

So, find a quiet place, get out your paints and brushes and spend some time in the commpany of some of nature's beautiful botanicals.

Gouache

(pronounced gwash)

Gouache is an opaque watercolor. The pigments are bound by a liquid glue, like Gum Arabic, and white pigment or chalk is added for more opacity. It has an almost suede like finish and lines painted with gouache can be very sharp. The colors can be brilliant or very subtle. It has a centuries old history and has been used for anything from illuminated manuscripts to modern commercial advertising work.

There are many brands of gouache available. I use mostly Winsor & Newton because it's easy to find and of good quality. Other brands are M. Graham, Holbein, Schmincke and Daler Rowney.

The first time you use gouache squeeze a small amount of color onto your palette. Even though you don't use it all up right away you'll be able to reconstitute it with water for later use. The only time this won't work is when you have a large area to cover. Use fresh paint for that or you'll get little lumps of undisolved paint in your piece. If that happens brush them off and touch up.

Don't add a lot of water to the paint, or fill up the paint well on your palette with water. Water is added to the paint a little at a time by dipping your brush in water and then working it into one side of your spot of paint. The paint should have a creamy consistency. If you add too much water the paint will lose its opacity. One exception in these exercises is when we paint an underpainting. In this instance we use a thinner layer of paint to cover the white of the paper before painting the top layers. The colors can be mixed in another well on the palette or, sometimes, directly on the painting.

One of the great advantages of gouache is that it's very "forgiving." If you find that a certain area is not working just paint over it and start again.

Start by squeezing out spots of paint about this size

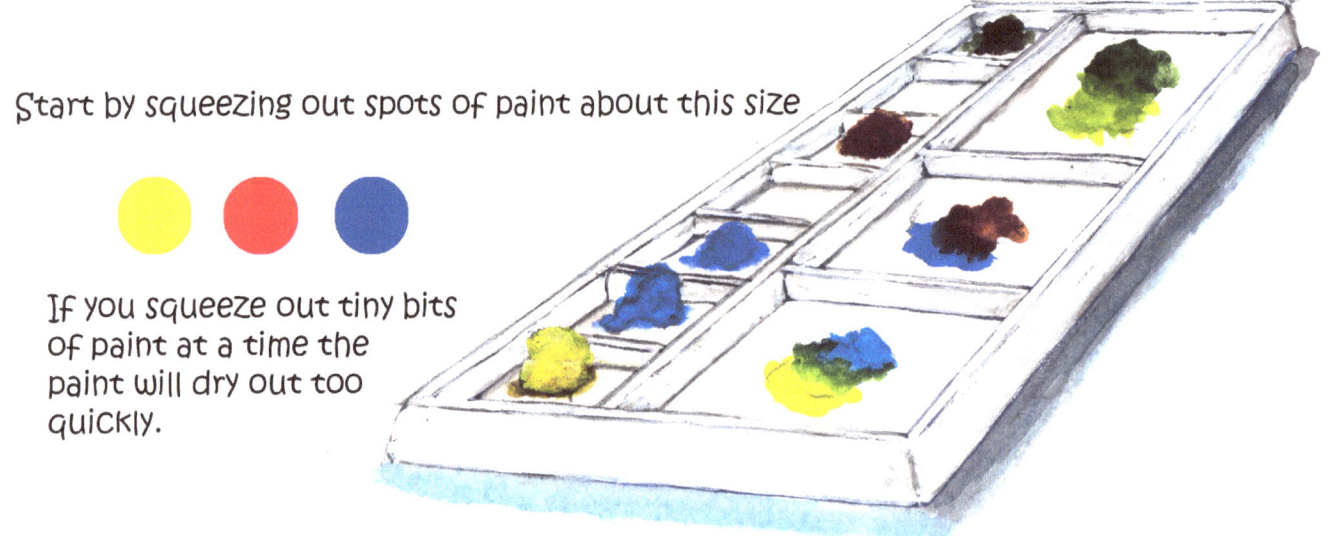

If you squeeze out tiny bits of paint at a time the paint will dry out too quickly.

Materials List
Botanical Illustration in Gouache
The Four Seasons

PENCILS -- I generally use a softer pencil, like a 4B, to draw with but use whatever you're comfortable with. Just make sure that you don't make your marks so hard that they're hard to erase. I use a kneaded eraser because it won't leave little crumbly bits of material that have to be brushed off.

PAPER -- I recommend using hot press watercolor paper, preferably 140 #, although a little lighter weight would be OK, too. Some artists use illustration board, vellum or bristol. I use Arches 140# hot press because it has a nice, smooth surface to make detailing easier and crisper looking. Experiment and try some different papers. One half standard size sheet should be plenty for this course.

PALETTE -- It should be white so you can see exactly what color you're mixing. If you don't have a palette a white paper plate works fine. It's just a little harder to transport wet paint if you have to move around. Its always nice to have one that closes, too.

WATER CONTAINER -- Use whatever you have on hand. At home I use old plastic cat food containers (thoroughly washed!) -- no breakage problem.

TRANSFER PAPER -- Depending on how you transfer your images you may or may not need some plain tracing paper. An 11" x 14" sheet folded in half should do. Cover one side completely with soft graphite.

BRUSHES -- You'll probably need three small watercolor brushes: a 4/0 small round, a #1 small round and a very small either 18/0 or 20/0 round.

GOUACHE -- The ten tubes listed here will give you enough variety of colors to complete all the illustrations in this course. The brand I use is Winsor & Newton but that's not a requirement.

Permanent White	Yellow Ochre
Marigold Yellow	Olive Green
Burnt Umber	Ultramarine Blue
Burnt Sienna	Brilliant Yellow
Spectrum Red	Opera Pink or Bengal Rose

About This Course

A few words about drawing -- Drawing is one of the backbones of illustration. Practice! Practice! Practice! Try to do a little drawing every day and it doesn't have to be anything like a finished piece of art. Draw stick figures. Draw your coffee mug. Keep a pen and paper by your favorite chair and when you find yourself trapped there with a cat on your lap (COL) draw what you see around you. Sweep your lines. Squiggle your lines. It all goes toward training your brain to direct your hand to make marks. Having said that, this course is not a drawing class so you'll be starting out the demonstrations with the subjects already drawn for you so you can transfer them to your watercolor paper and then follow along as the illustration is developed.

Throughout this course you'll see the word "blend" over and over again. I can't stress enough how important it is to learn this technique. If your strokes aren't blended a bit they'll look too hard edged and your subject won't look realistic. The first exercise is geared toward practicing blending.
After you make your strokes, take a damp brush and gently run it over the strokes, parallel to them, to soften them and blend the color into the layer underneath them. This will also change the color. I always have a paper towel in the hand that's not holding the paint brush so I can dry off the excess water before I touch my brush to the paper.

A note about color: Don't worry about getting exactly the same colors as in the demonstrations. Color can be fleeting. Look at a flower on a cloudy day and then look at the same one shining in the sun. One day it could be a dull gray and the next a brilliant, eye stopping bright blue. There's not always a "right" color.

Pay attention to the values in your paintings. Value is the lightness or darkness of your paint, and without a good range of values your painting will look a bit boring, without, well. . . sparkle! Some samples of value scales are below.

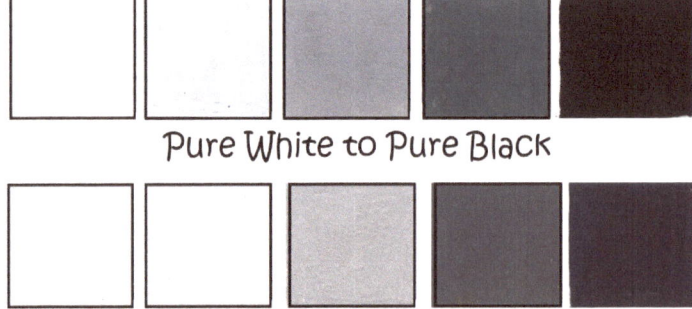

Pure White to Pure Black

Burnt Umber/Ultramarine Blue: light to dark

Before You Begin

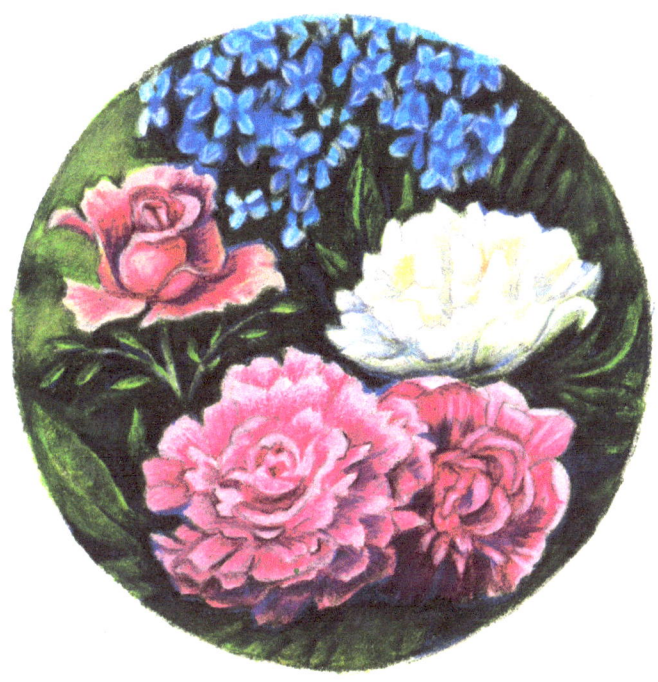

Here are a few tips on health and safety.

BE AWARE! Some of the pigments we work with are poisonous. Visit a site like http://sis.nim.gov/enviro/arthazards.html for specific information on the pigments or processes you use.

For this course please remember three things.

1. Don't put the tips of your brushes in your mouth!

2. Wash your hands after painting before you eat.

3. Get up and stretch frequently. Besides loosening up your body you'll come back to your painting with fresh eyes and it will be easier to see the progress you've made and what has yet to be done.

Blending Exercise
Acorn

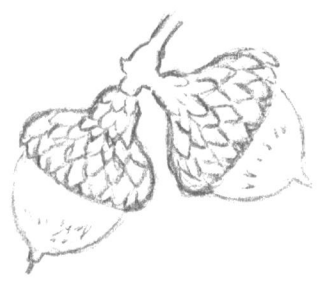

This first short exercise is designed
to give you practice in the all
important technique of blending.

Use this sheet to transfer
the image to a sheet
of watercolor paper.

Acorn

Colors Used: Yellow Ochre, Permanent White, Ultramarine Blue, Burnt Sienna, Burnt Umber

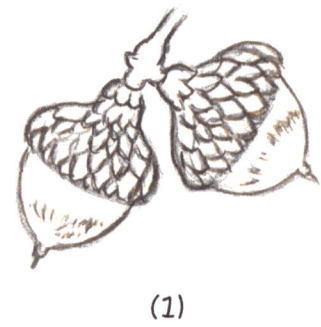

(1)

After you transfer the acorn image to your watercolor paper, lightly go over your pencil lines with Burnt Umber so you don't lose them when you start layering on gouache.

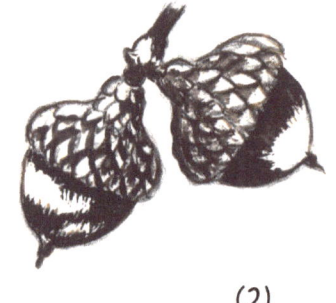

(2)

With Burnt Umber mixed with Ultramarine Blue, paint in the darkest areas of the acorn.

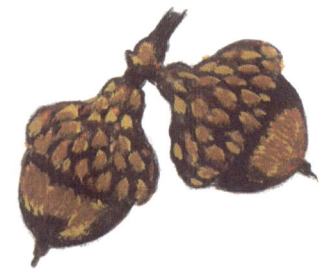

(3)

With a mixture of Yellow Ochre and Burnt Sienna, paint over the remaining white areas of the acorns.

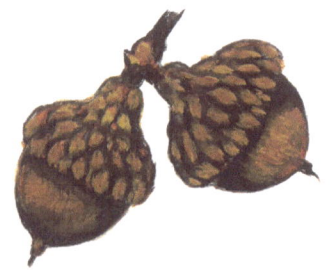

(4)

With a slightly damp brush, blend the medium values you made by mixing Burnt Sienna and Yellow Ochre into the dark values. If you blend too much, just add more of the medium or dark mixture and reblend. You want to soften the edges between the values so there's a smooth transition between them.

Acorn

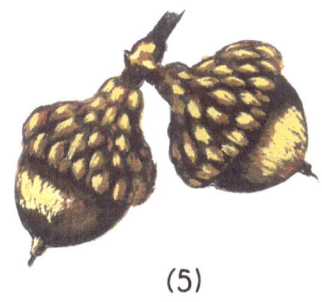

(5)

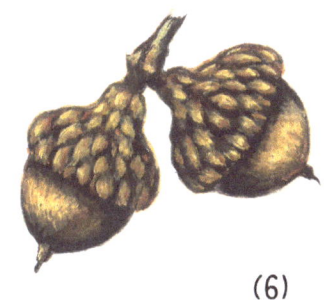

(6)

Use a mixture of Yellow Ochre and White to paint in the highlights on the acorns.

With a slightly damp brush, blend the edges of the lighter values so they make a smooth transition into the darker values. Don't blend the lighter value away entirely. If you do, just add more of the Yellow Ochre and White mixture and reblend. Always keep a paper towel in your hand not holding the brush. After you dip your brush in water, squeeze out most of the moisture before you blend. If you get the painting too wet the colors will run together.

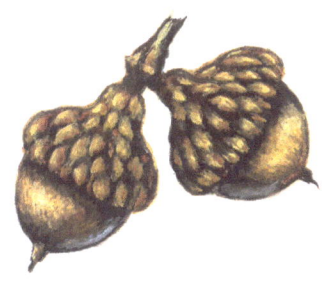

(7)

Mix White with Ultramarine Blue and paint a subtle arc of reflected light on the lower side of the acorns. Gently blend them in. With White, make a tiny highlight on the upper shiny portion of the nuts. Blend. With a damp brush, gently soften the outside edges of the acorns so they won't look pasted on the page.

Stand back and review your illustration. Adjust the values as needed. If you don't have a good range of values the painting will be dull and not as interesting to the eye as it will be with good contrast.

Spring

Winter Aconite
Eranthis hyemalis

This plant is one of the earliest bloomers in the spring. What a joy it is to see its cheery yellow flowers pushing through the snow after a long winter.

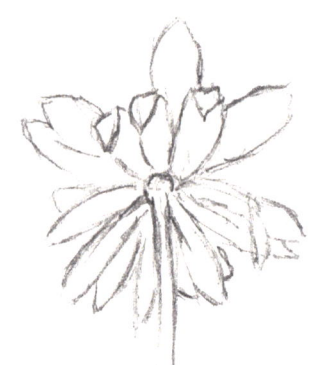

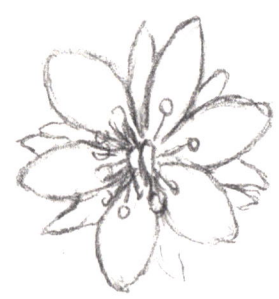

Although I've shown 3 views of the Aconite here, the demonstration is only for the center illustration showing the whold plant. Use what you learn from the demo to paint in the other two views. The last page of the Winter Aconite demo also shows more views. Try your hand at drawing them and then painting them using what you've learned in this demo.

Use this sheet to transfer the image to a sheet of watercolor paper.

Winter Aconite

Colors Used: Yellow Ochre, Permanent White, Ultramarine Blue, Olive Green, Burnt Umber, Brilliant Yellow

(1)

After you transfer the drawing of the Aconite to your watercolor paper, make sure your lines are dark enough so they'll still show when you begin layering on gouache. If they're not, go over them with a very thin line of Burnt Umber.

STEM -- The stems are pale green at the top and almost white toward the bottom. With White tinted with a little Olive Green, start painting the stems. As you go down the stem add more and more White.

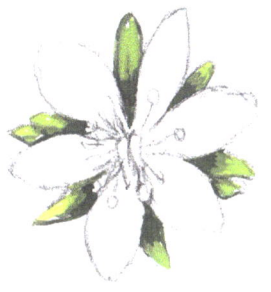

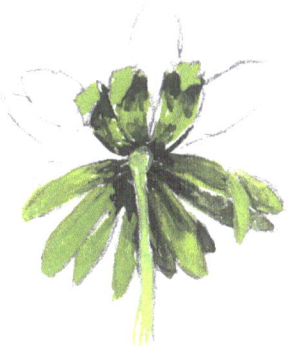

ROOT Ball -- Paint the ball with a mixture of Burnt Sienna and Burnt Umber. Use a mixture of White slightly tinted with Burnt Umber and Ultramarine Blue to paint the pale roots.

LEAVES around the flower head (inflourescence) -- With a mixture of Olive Green, Burnt Umber and Ultramarine Blue, paint the dark portions of the leaves closest to the center. With a mixture of Olive Green, Primary Yellow and White, paint the ends of the leaves.

Winter Aconite

(2)

STEMS --With a dark mixture of Burnt Umber and Ultramarine Blue, paint a shadow on the right side of the stems. With White tinted with Brilliant Yellow paint a highlight on the left side of the stems toward the top.

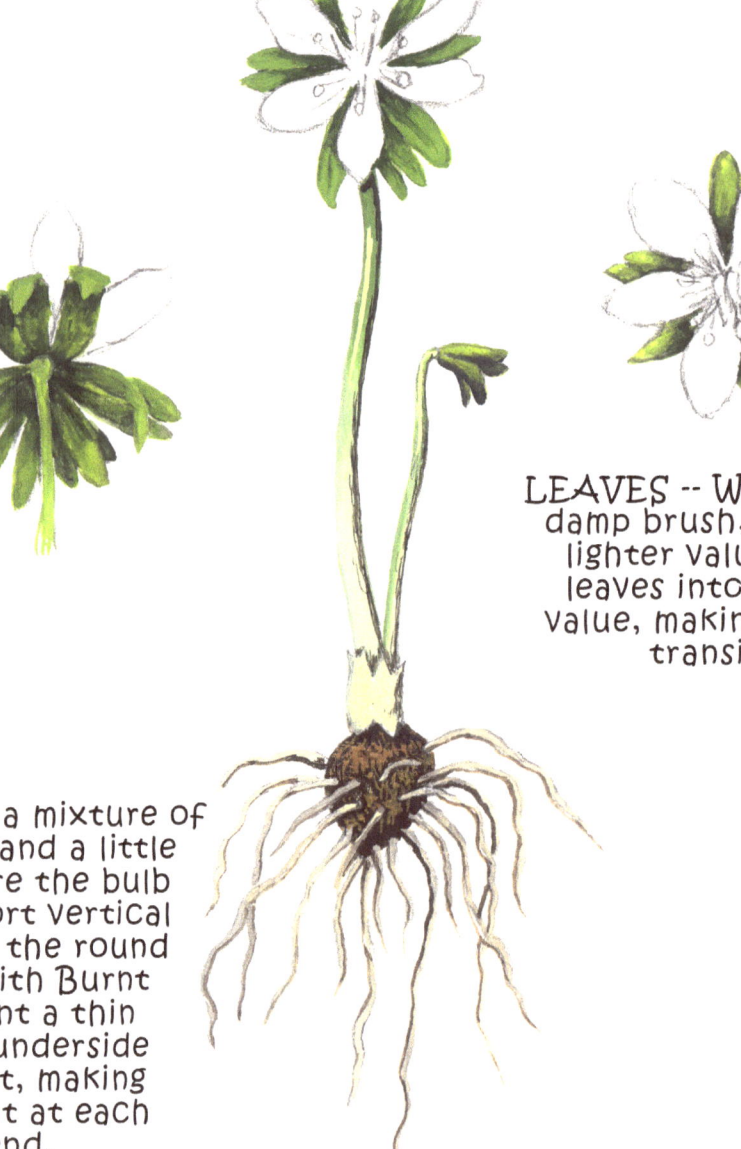

LEAVES -- With a slightly damp brush, blend the lighter values on the leaves into the dark value, making a smooth transition.

ROOTS -- With a mixture of Burnt Sienna and a little White, texture the bulb by making short vertical lines folloring the round contour. With Burnt Umber, paint a thin line on the underside of each root, making a sharp point at each root end.

Winter Aconite

(3)

STEMS --With a slightly damp brush,
gently blend the shadows and highlights
into the first layer you painted on the
stems. Make sure the transition
between the values is smooth.
You may have to add more of the
light or dark values and reblend
to get the right effect.

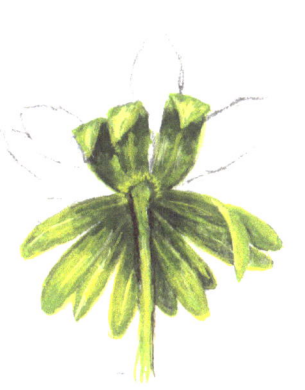

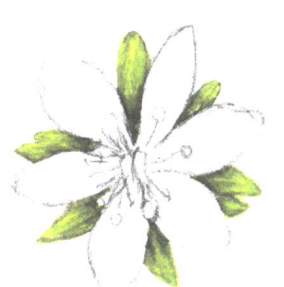

LEAVES -- With a mixture of White
and Brilliant Yellow, paint
the highlights on the leaves.

BULB -- With a slightly damp
brush, blend the lighter Burnt
Sienna mixture a little. You
may have to add more of the
lighter or darker value if you
lose too much of them. Be
sure to keep some texture
showing. Add a tiny bit of
White to Yellow Ochre and
paint a highlight on the upper
portion of the bulb. Blend.

ROOTS -- With a slightly
damp brush, blend the dark
shadow line into the off
white color. You may have
to keep adding White and
reblending if the root gets
too dark. Also, soften the
outside edges of the roots
so they don't look pasted
on the paper.

13

Winter Aconite

(4)

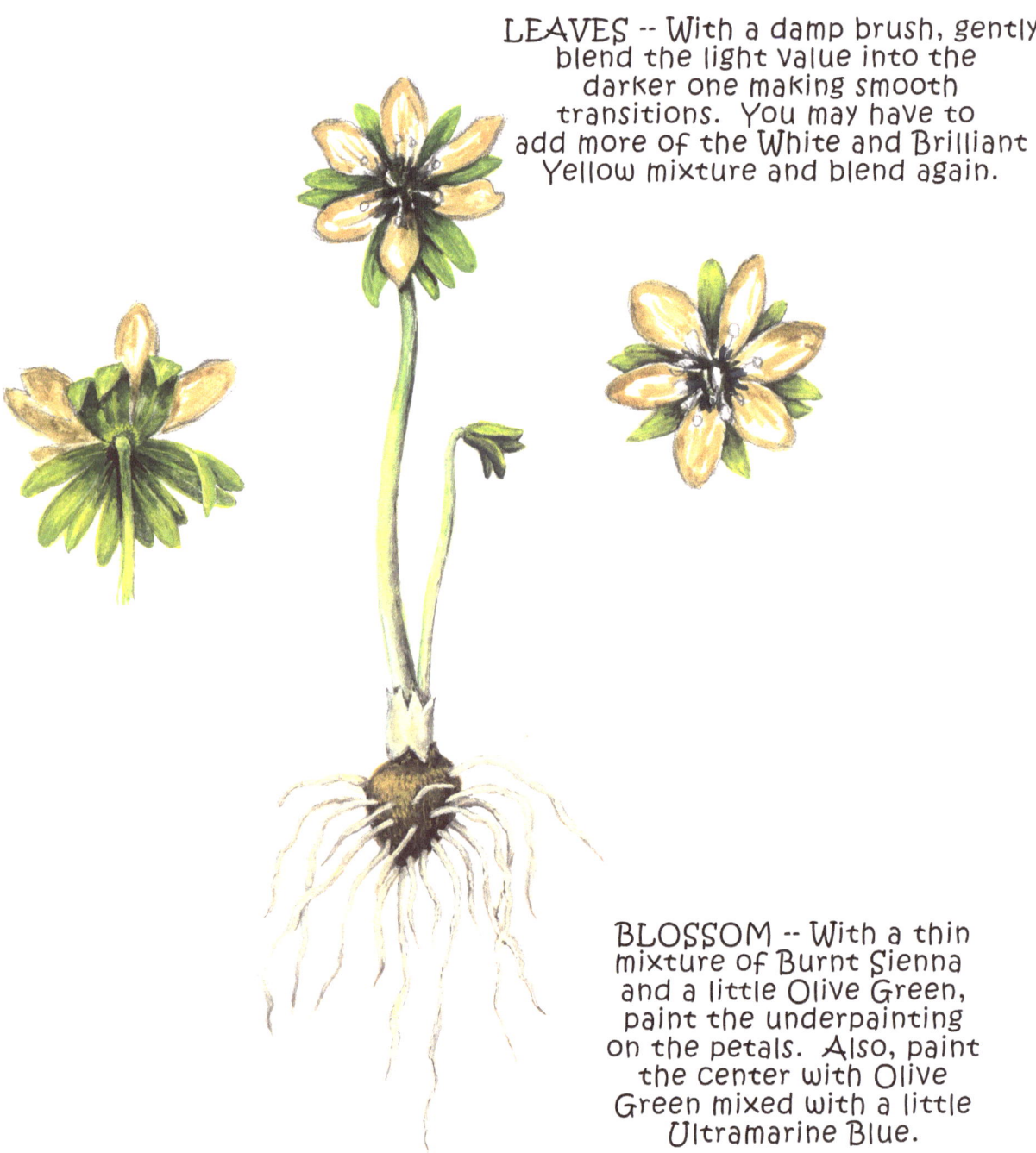

LEAVES -- With a damp brush, gently blend the light value into the darker one making smooth transitions. You may have to add more of the White and Brilliant Yellow mixture and blend again.

BLOSSOM -- With a thin mixture of Burnt Sienna and a little Olive Green, paint the underpainting on the petals. Also, paint the center with Olive Green mixed with a little Ultramarine Blue.

Winter Aconite

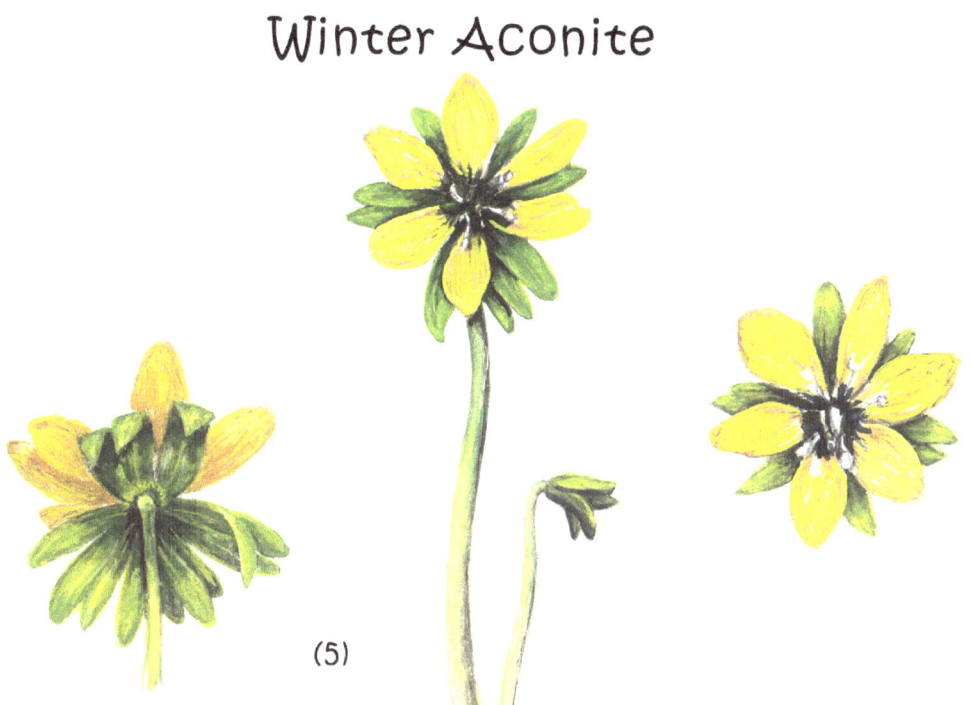

(5)

BLOSSOM -- With thick Brilliant Yellow tinted with a little White, paint the petals. Make your strokes go from the center of the flower outwards to the edges. Paint right up to the edges, leaving only a hair's breadth of the Burnt Sienna underpainting showing.

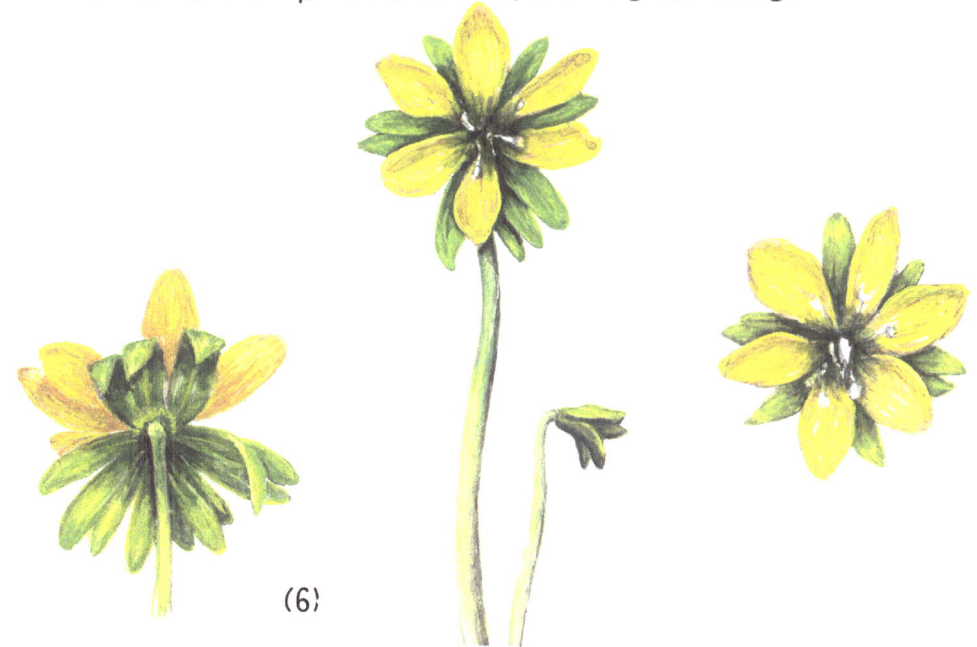

(6)

BLOSSOM -- With a slightly damp brush, blend the edges where the Yellow of the petals and the dark center meet to soften them. You'll be painting the center elements over the dark center and not much of it will be showing in the finished painting. Also, using a thin wash of Burnt Sienna and Olive Green, paint subtle shadows on the petals. Blend their edges to soften them.

Winter Aconite

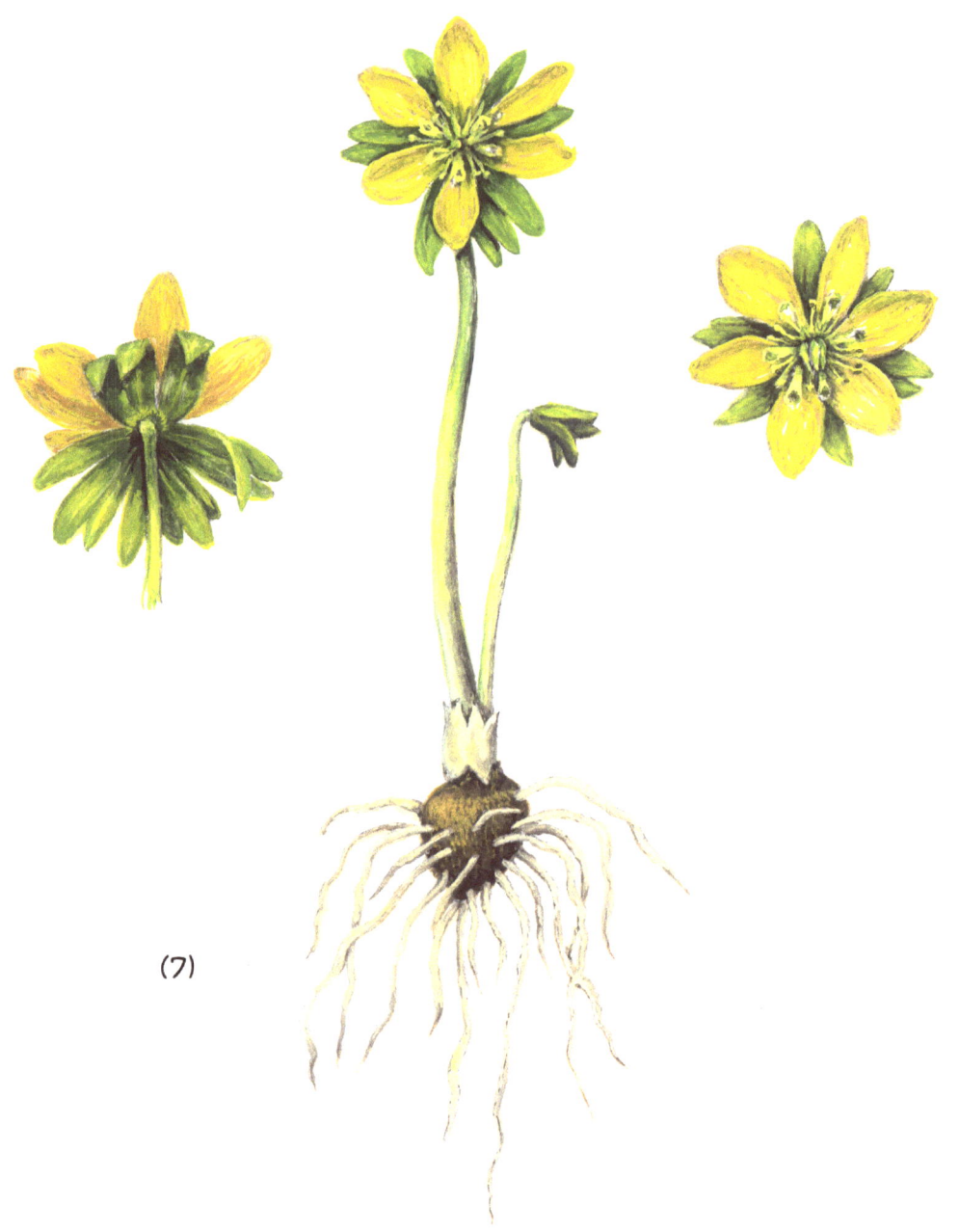

(7)

THE CENTER --The center of the Aconite is intricate so look very carefully.
The center detailing is done with Brilliant Yellow with a little White added.
Be sure to blend the ends of the stamens where they emerge from the
flower's center so they darken and fade into the shadows.

Now, stand back and look at your illustration. Make sure that the outside
edges are softened so the flower won't look pasted on the paper. Make any
needed adjustments in value. If you don't have a good range of lights and
darks the flower won't "pop" from the page. You might want to come back
to your painting in a couple of days and reevaluate.

Winter Aconite

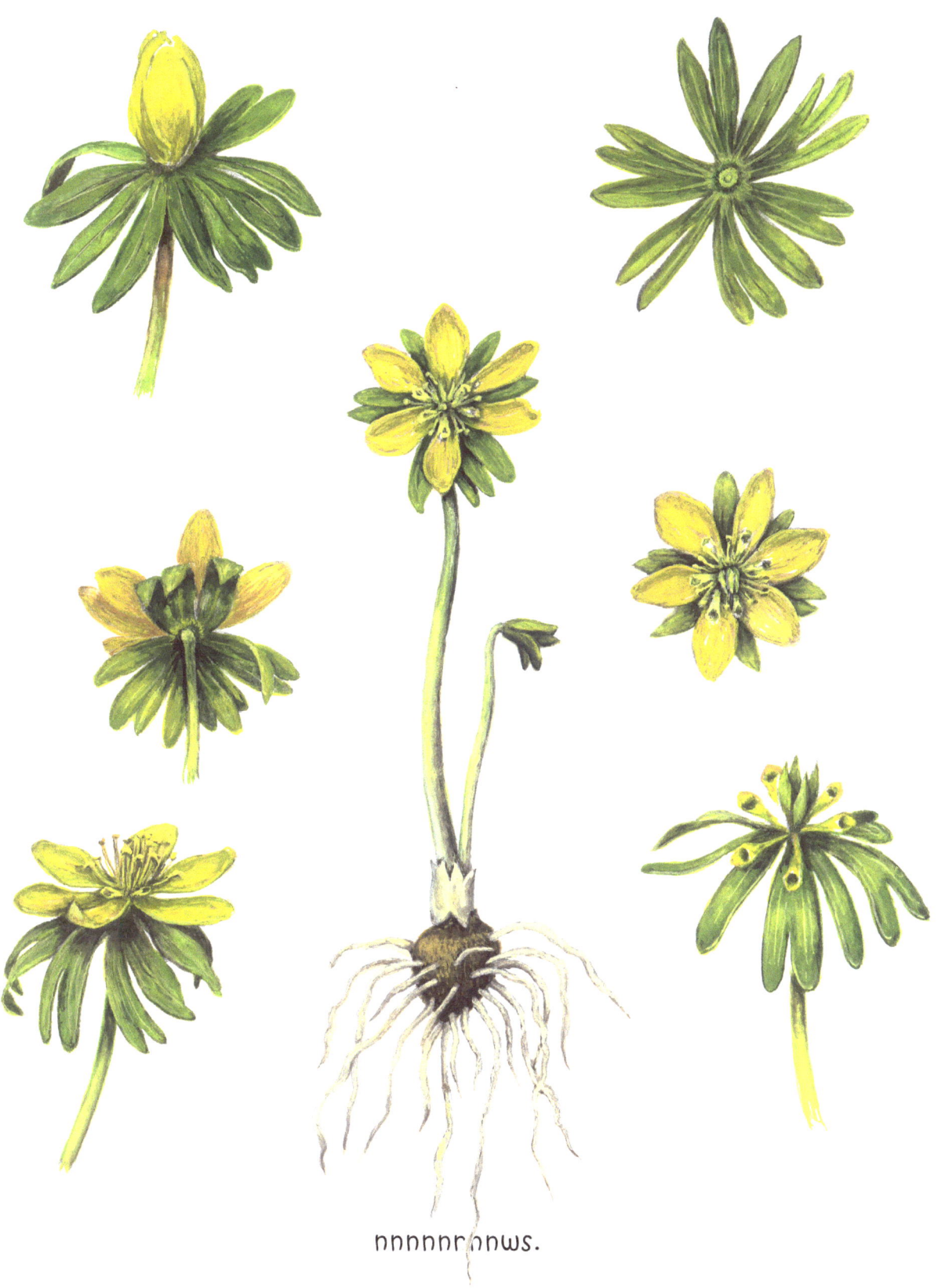

nnnnnrnnws.

Summer
Wild Bergamot/Monarda/Bee Balm
Monarda fistulosa
(This plant is known by several common names)

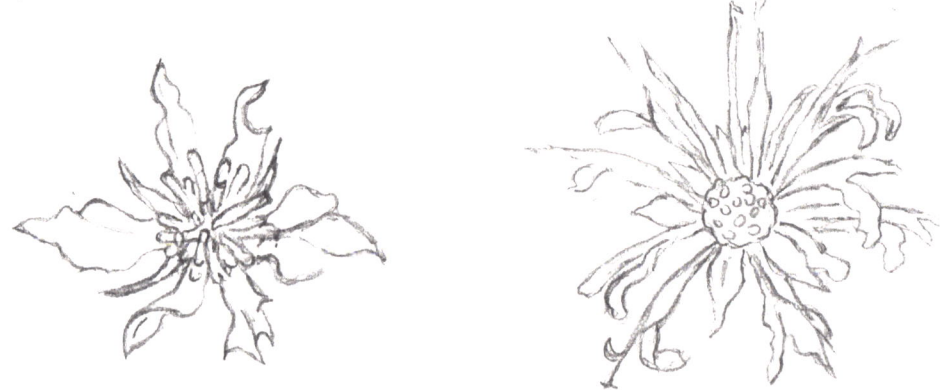

Use this sheet to transfer
the image to a sheet
of watercolor paper.

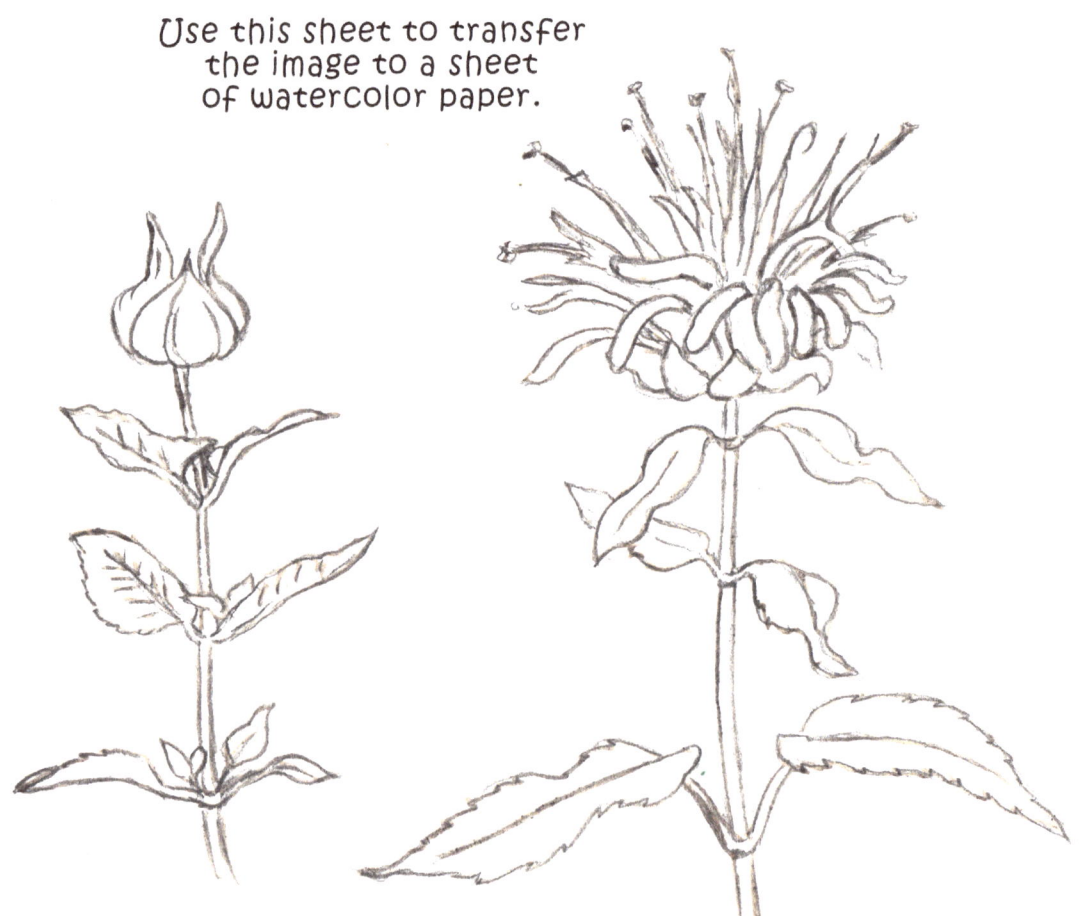

I can remember my Grandmother showing us children how
to pull out each individual flower segment to suck out
the little drop of sweetness from the end. This flower
is a hummingbird favorite.

The demonstration shows the steps to complete the
lower two illustrations. The same techniques can
be used to complete the painting of the two upper drawings.

18

Wild Bergamot

Colors Used: Permanent White, Ulltramarine Blue,
Olive Green, Burnt Umber, BrilliantYellow, Spectrum Red,
Opera Pink or Bengal Rose (Bengal Rose has been discontinued
but you may have it in your kit)

(1)

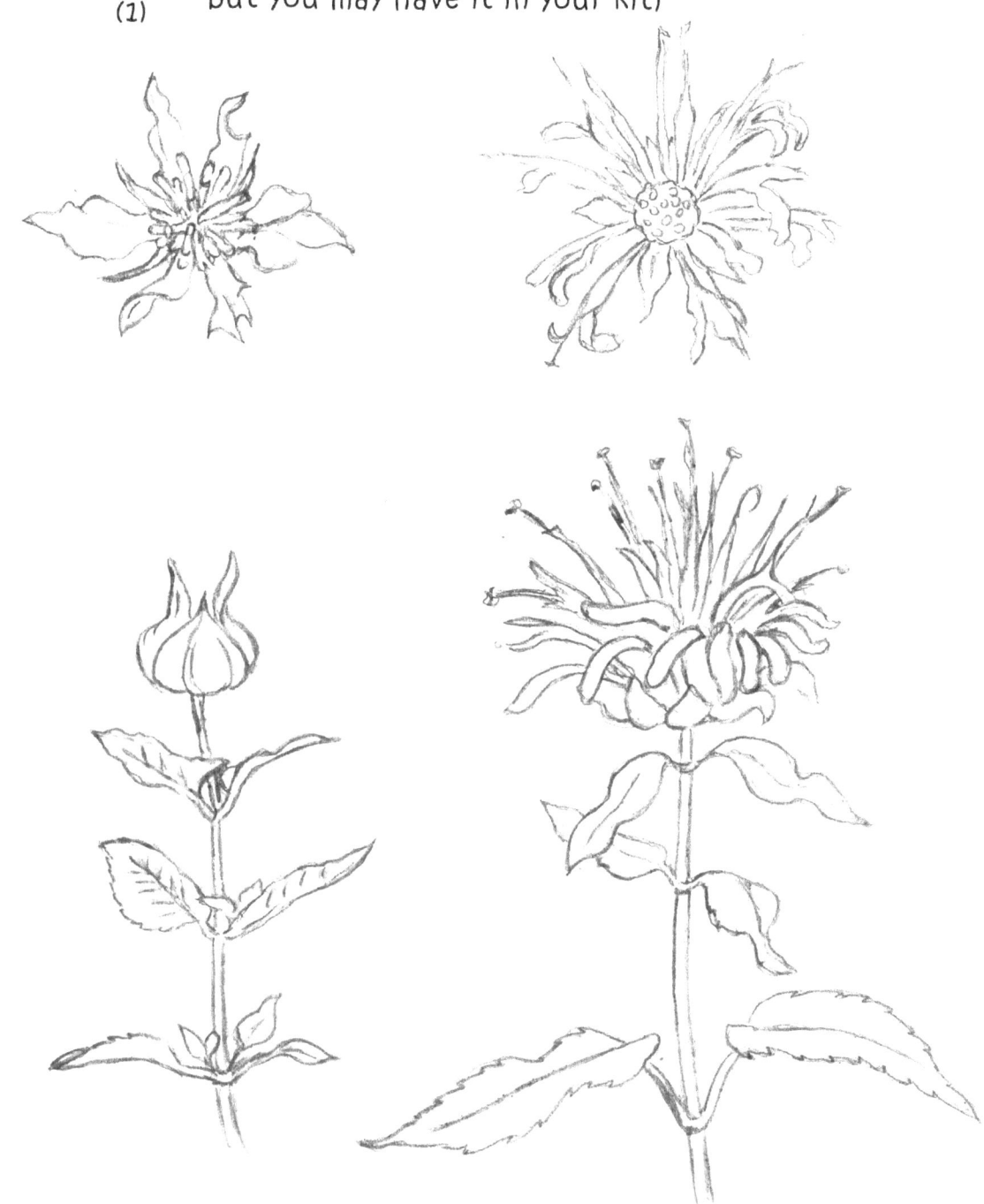

Transfer the drawing to watercolor paper and go over the lines with a thin
wash of Burnt Umber. Make the lines very thin. You just want to set your
lines. If you make the lines too wide the dark color will interfere with the
upper layers. If your pencil lines are dark enough you can skip this step.

Wild Bergamot

(2)

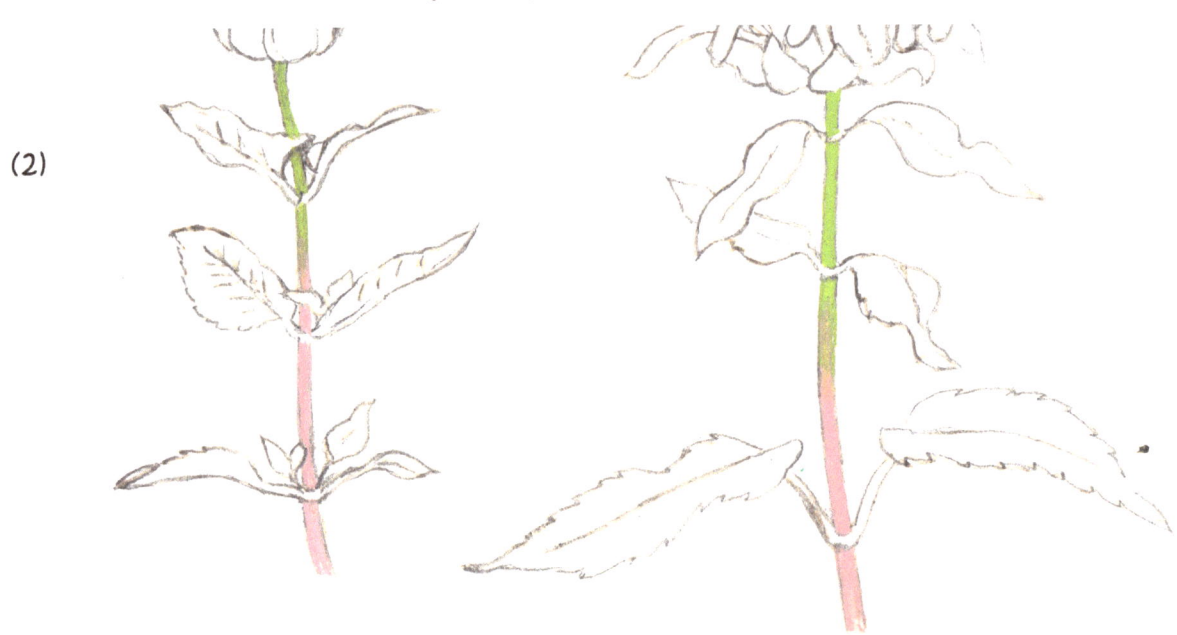

THE STEMS -- The stems are green at the top and a pinkish brown at the bottom. Use Olive Green mixed with White and a little Brilliant Yellow to paint the top section of the stems. Add White to Spectrum Red to paint the bottom of the stems. Use a damp brush to blend the two colors where they meet.

(3)

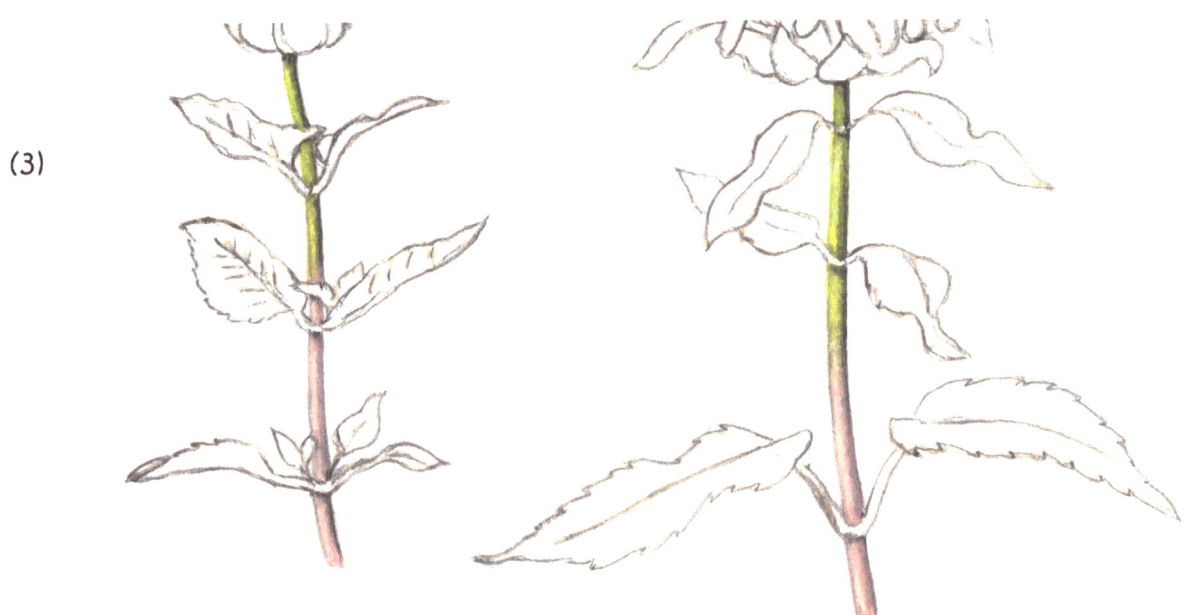

With a dark mixture of Burnt Umber and Ultramarine Blue, paint a very thin line on the shadow (right side) of the stems. With a damp brush, gently blend the dark line into the previous layer of gouache. With a light value mixture of White plus a little Brilliant Yellow, paint a highlight on the upper stem on the left side. Paint a highlight, using pure White on the lower left side. With a damp brush, gently blend the highlights into the previous layers. The transition between the colors should be smooth and the stems should look rounded.

Wild Bergamot

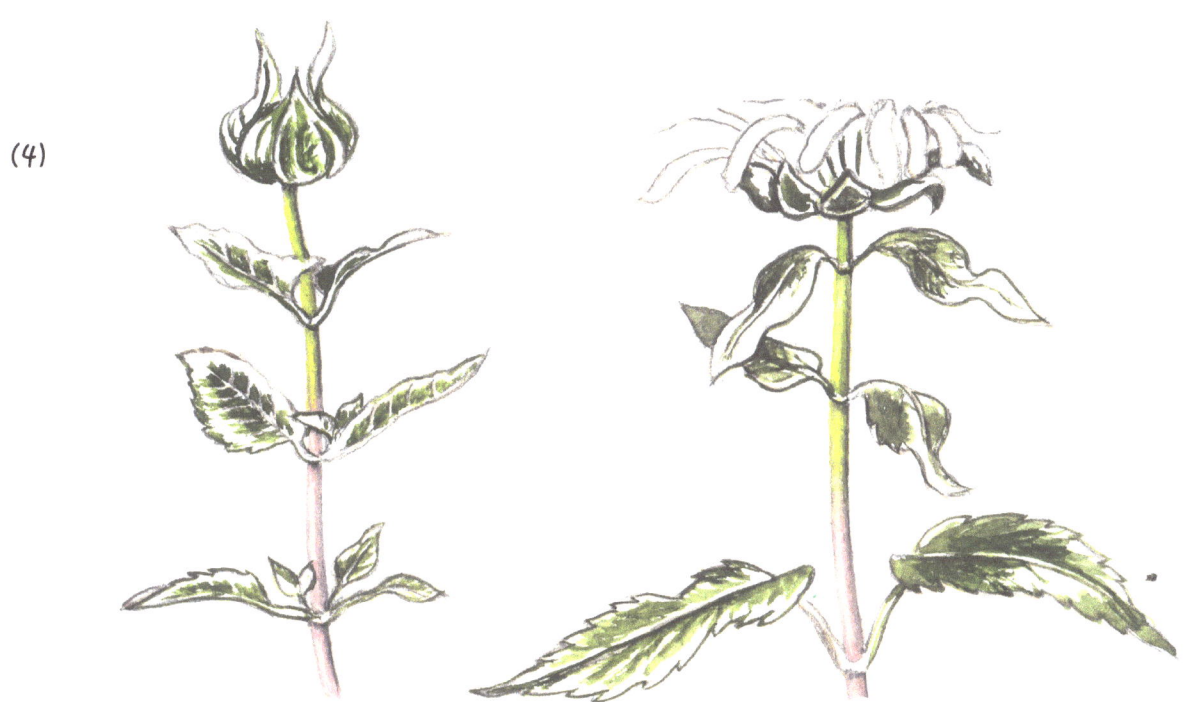

(4)

LEAVES and BUD -- With a mixture of Olive Green tinted with a little Burnt Umber and Ultramarine Blue, paint the darkest areas of the leaves and bud.

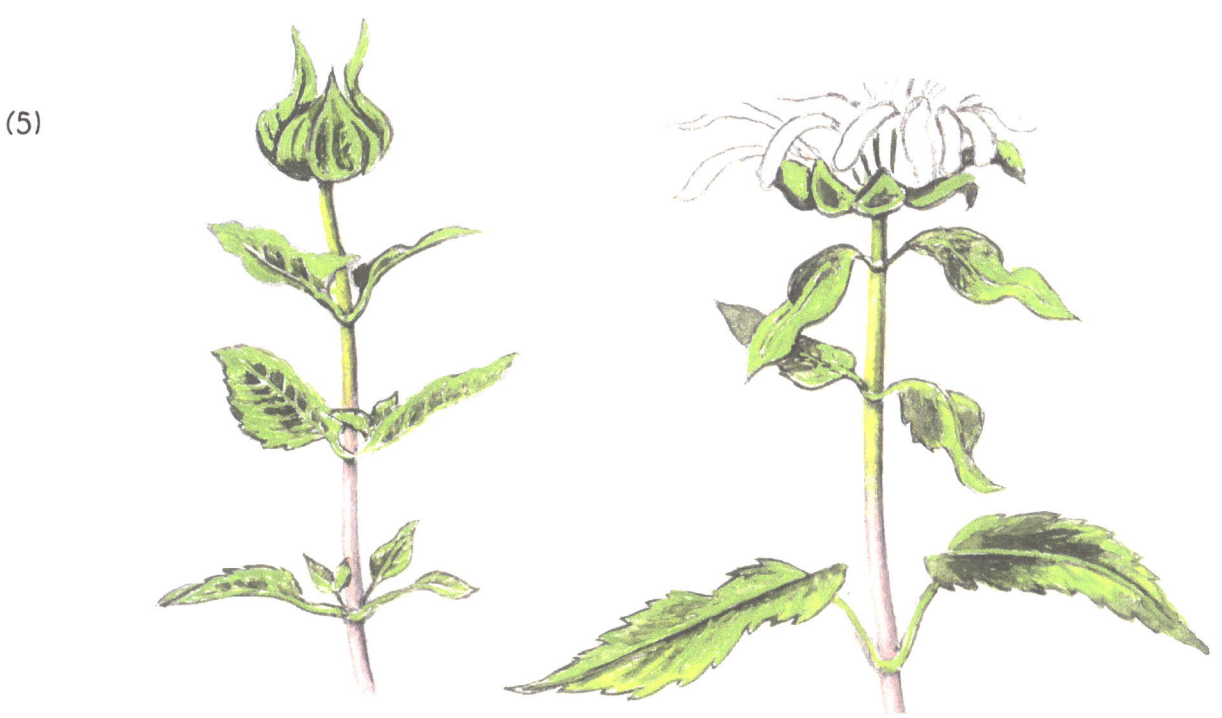

(5)

LeAVES and BUD - With a medium value mixture of Olive Green, Brilliant Yellow and White, paint in the rest of the leaves and bud.

Wild Bergamot

(6)

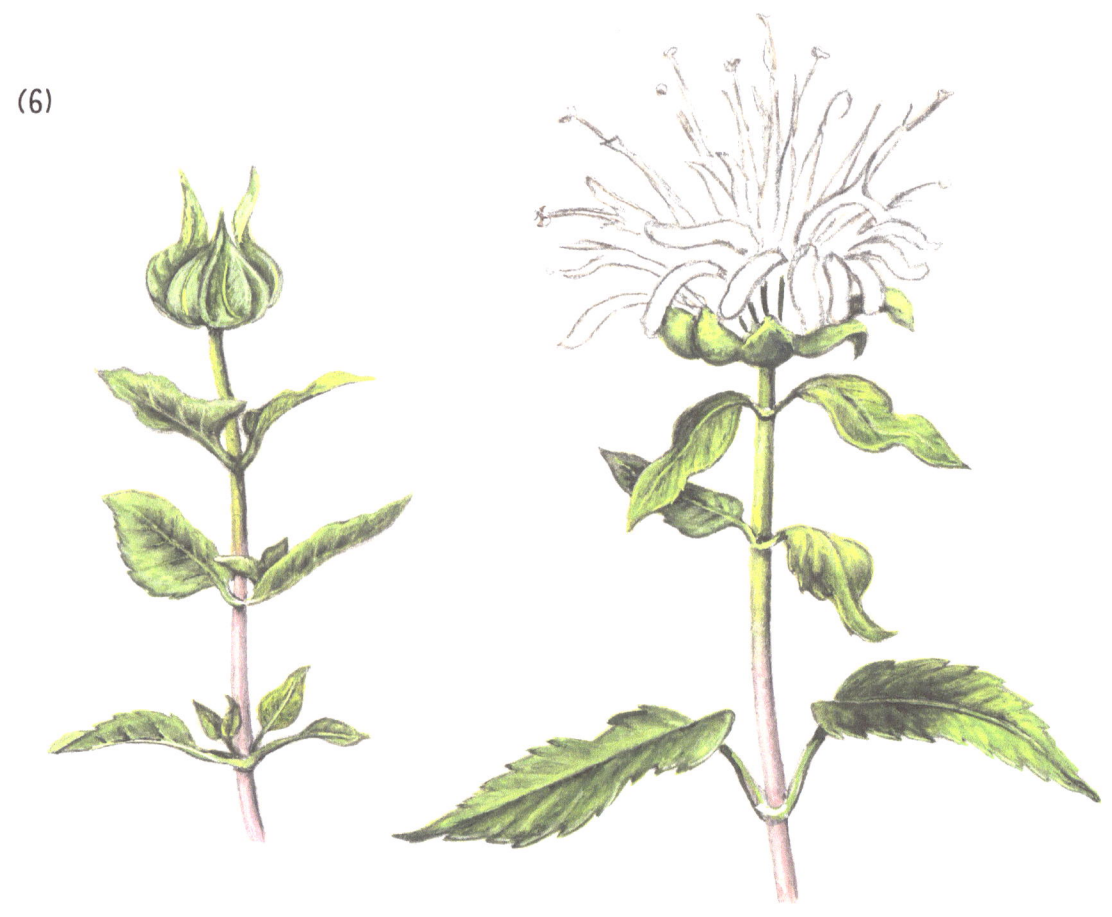

LEAVES and BUD -- With a slightly damp brush, begin blending the
medium value into the dark value. When the transition is
smooth, add highlights with pure White and gently
blend that in. If you lose too much of your dark value just paint
back in more of the Olive Green, Burnt Umber and Ultramarine
Blue mixture.. Reblend. You may have to add the highlights
and reblend several times, also. This is a back and forth
process. Paint a thin line of White along the front edges of the
leaves to give them dimension. Blend them in a little.
It took me several hours to paint these leaves.

Wild Bergamot

(7)

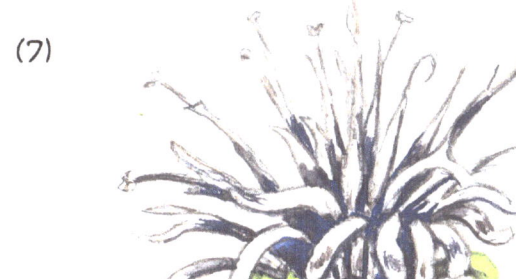

BLOSSOM -- (inflourescence) --
With a dark mixture of Burnt
Umber and Ultramarine Blue,
paint in the shadow areas on
the petals.

(8)

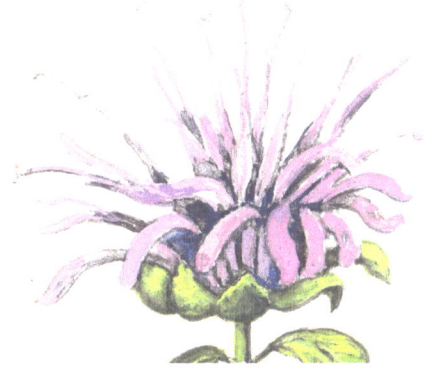

With a mixture of White tinted
with Ultramarine Blue and
Opera Pink (or Bengal Rose),
paint the rest of the petals.

(9)

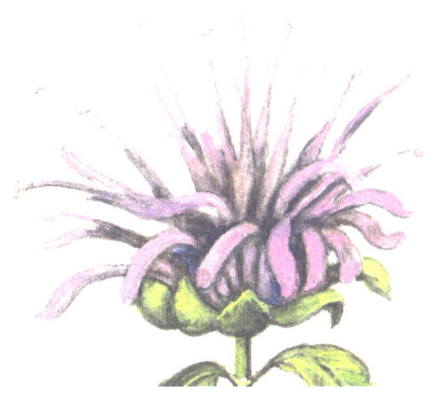

With a slightly damp brush,
blend the values together
where they meet, making
smooth transitions.

Wild Bergamot

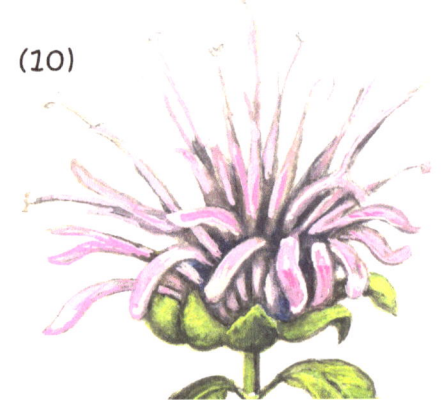

(10)

With a mixture of White barely tinted with Ultramarine Blue and Opera Pink (or Bengal Rose), paint highlights on each petal.

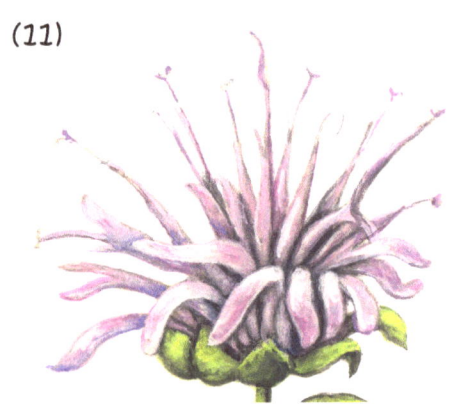

(11)

With a slightly damp brush, blend the highlights in a little to make smooth transitions between the values. If you lose too much of the lightest value repaint and blend again. Also, if you lose too much of the dark value, repaint it and blend again. This is a back and forth process.

Wild Bergamot

(12)

(13)

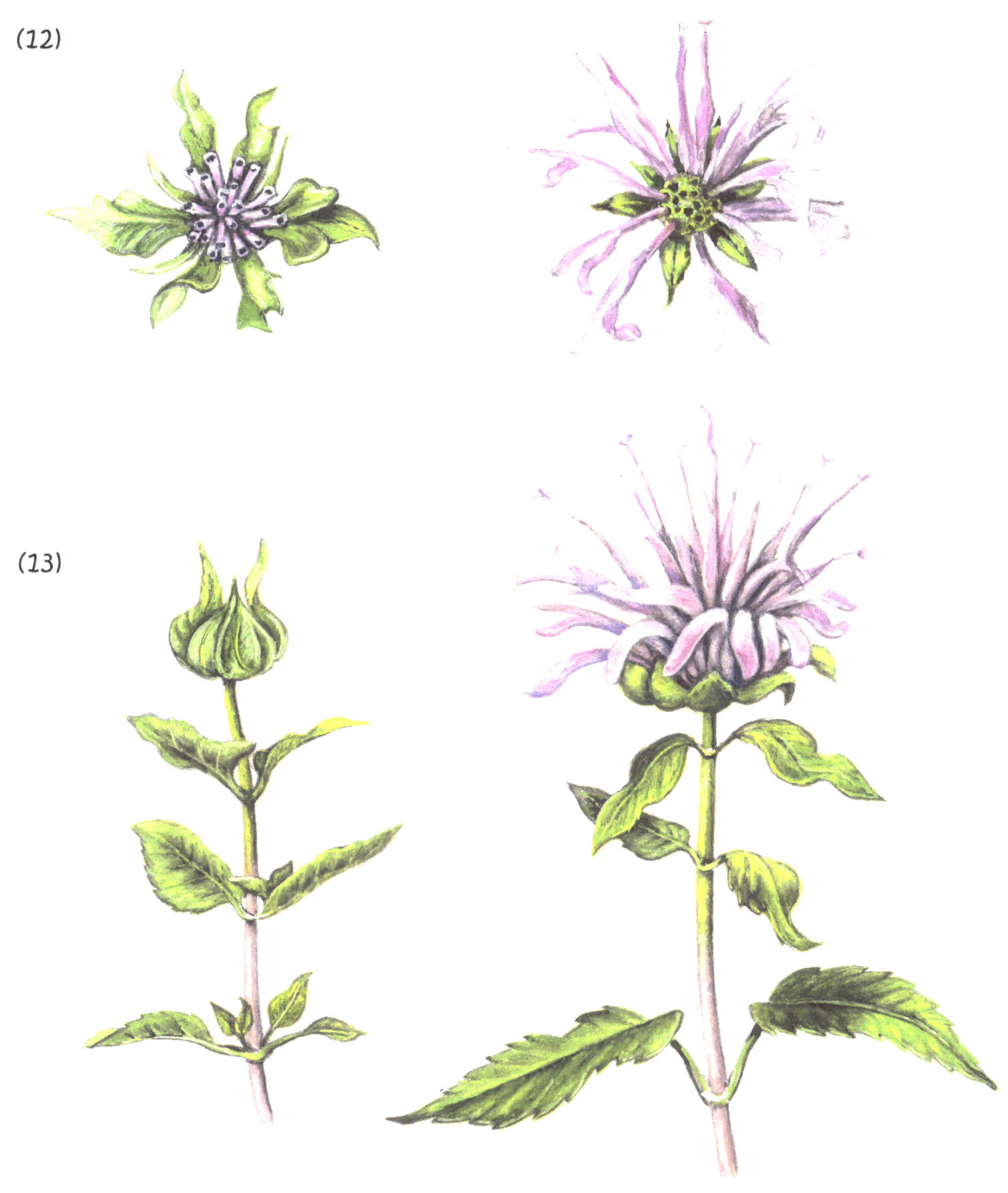

Autumn

Dewberry Leaves
Rubus flagellaris

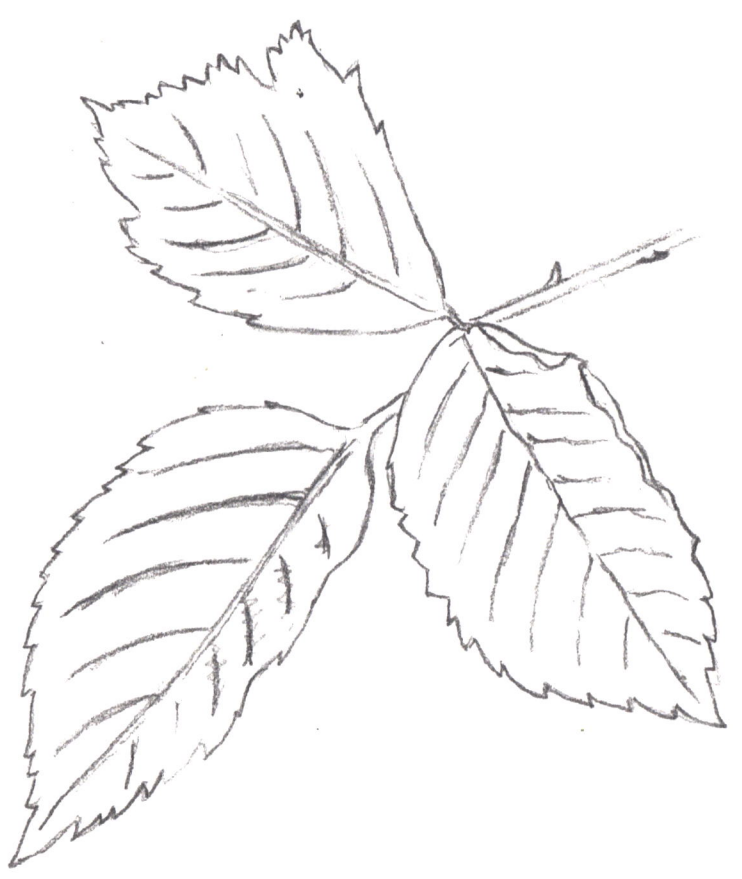

When the weather cools the Dewberry leaves
turn a stunning dark red that
glows on a sunny day.

Use this sheet to transfer
the image to a sheet
of watercolor paper.

26

Dewberry Leaves

Colors Used: Yellow Ochre, Marigold Yellow Ultramarine Blue,
Spectrum Red, Burnt Umber

(1)

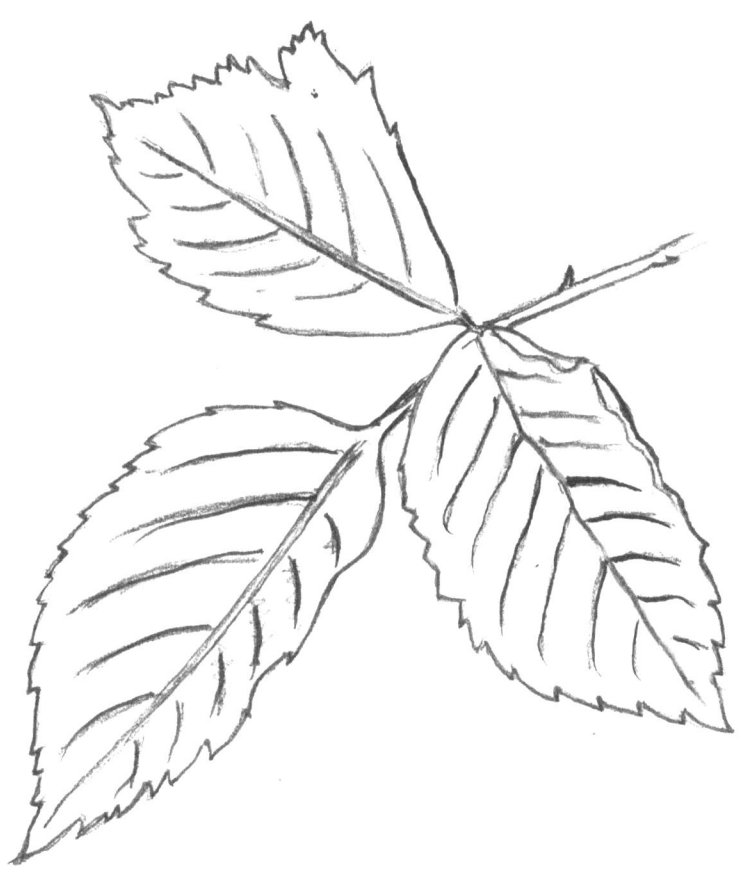

Transfer the drawing of the leaves to your
watercolor paper. Use a thin wash of Burnt
Umber to go over the lines so they're not lost
when you begin layering on gouache. If your
pencil lines are dark enough you can skip this step.

Dewberry Leaves

(2)

With a dark value of Burnt Umber mixed with Ultramarine Blue, paint in the dark areas on the leaves and stem.

(3)

Paint the rest of the leaves with Spectrum Red. Paint the stem with Yellow Ochre.

Dewberry Leaves

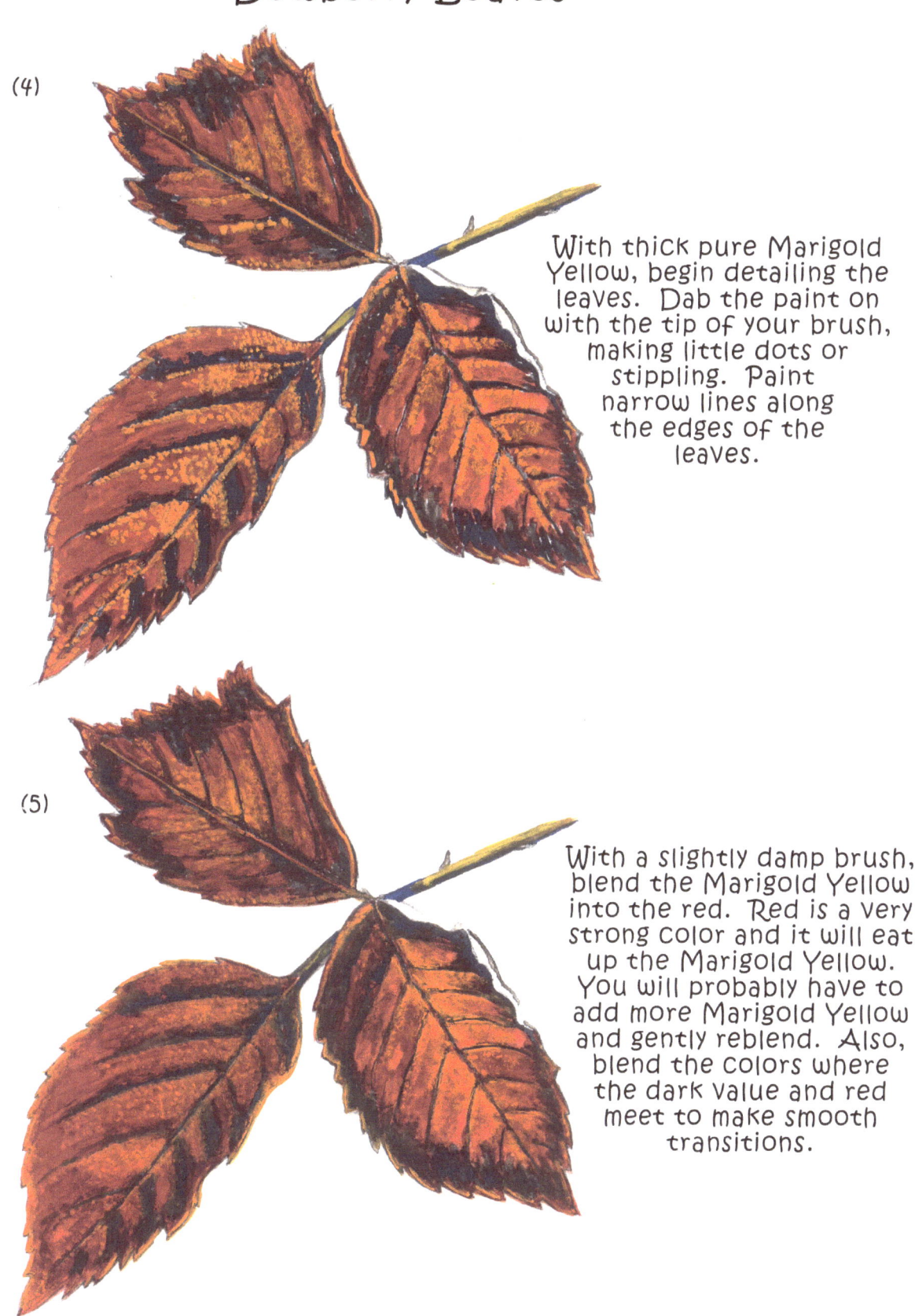

(4)

With thick pure Marigold Yellow, begin detailing the leaves. Dab the paint on with the tip of your brush, making little dots or stippling. Paint narrow lines along the edges of the leaves.

(5)

With a slightly damp brush, blend the Marigold Yellow into the red. Red is a very strong color and it will eat up the Marigold Yellow. You will probably have to add more Marigold Yellow and gently reblend. Also, blend the colors where the dark value and red meet to make smooth transitions.

Dewberry Leaves

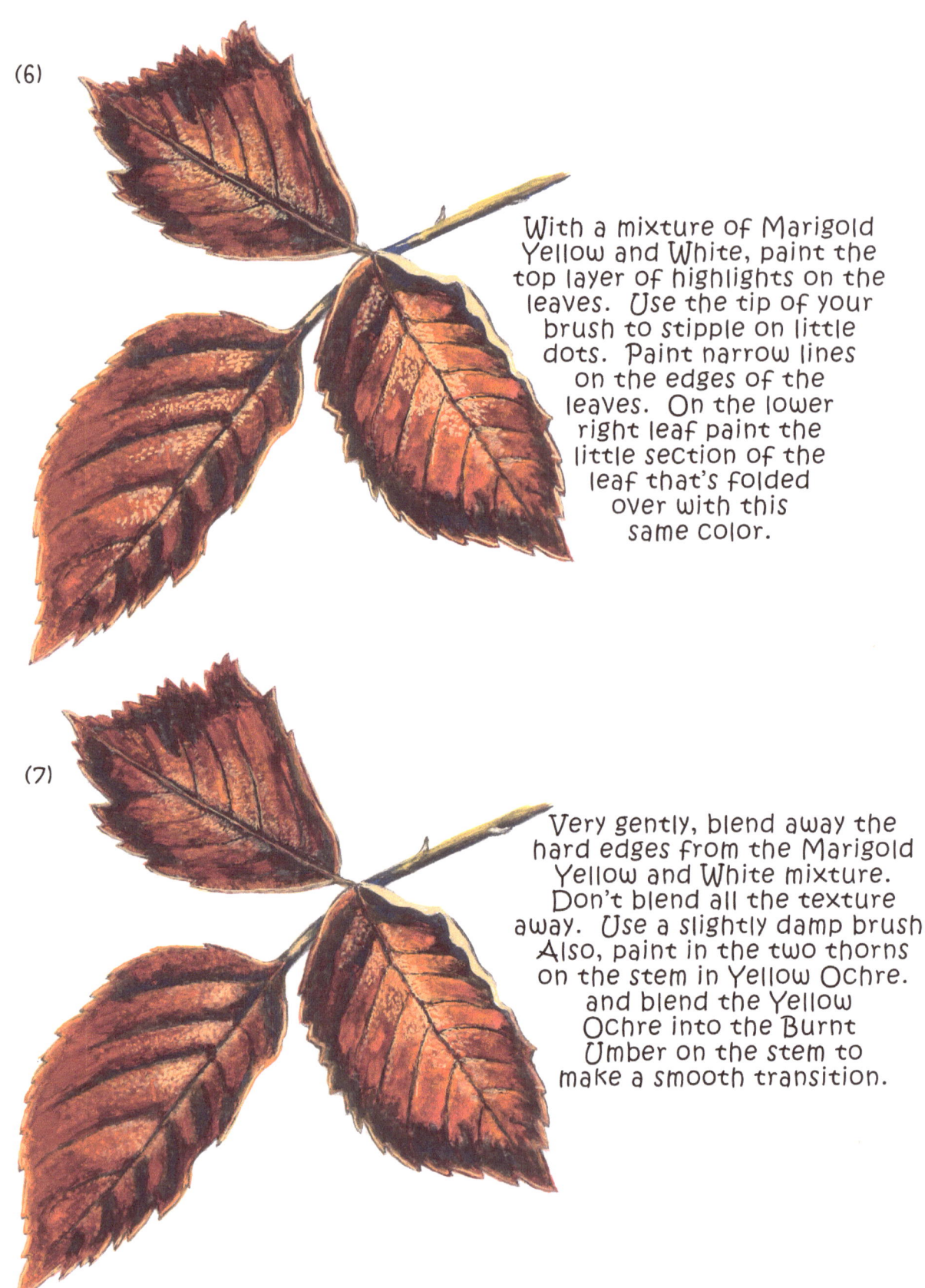

(6)

With a mixture of Marigold Yellow and White, paint the top layer of highlights on the leaves. Use the tip of your brush to stipple on little dots. Paint narrow lines on the edges of the leaves. On the lower right leaf paint the little section of the leaf that's folded over with this same color.

(7)

Very gently, blend away the hard edges from the Marigold Yellow and White mixture. Don't blend all the texture away. Use a slightly damp brush. Also, paint in the two thorns on the stem in Yellow Ochre. and blend the Yellow Ochre into the Burnt Umber on the stem to make a smooth transition.

Dewberry Leaves

(8)

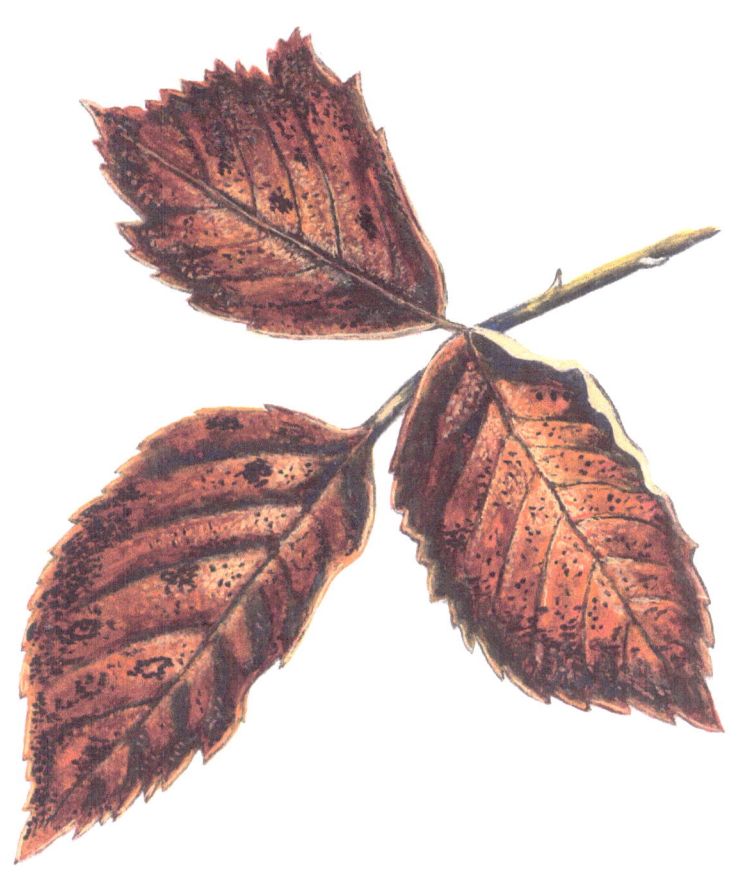

Using a dark value of Burnt and Ultramarine Blue, finish detailing the leaves. With the tip of your brush, stipple tiny dots to make the "imperfections" on the leaves.

Dewberry Leaves

(9)

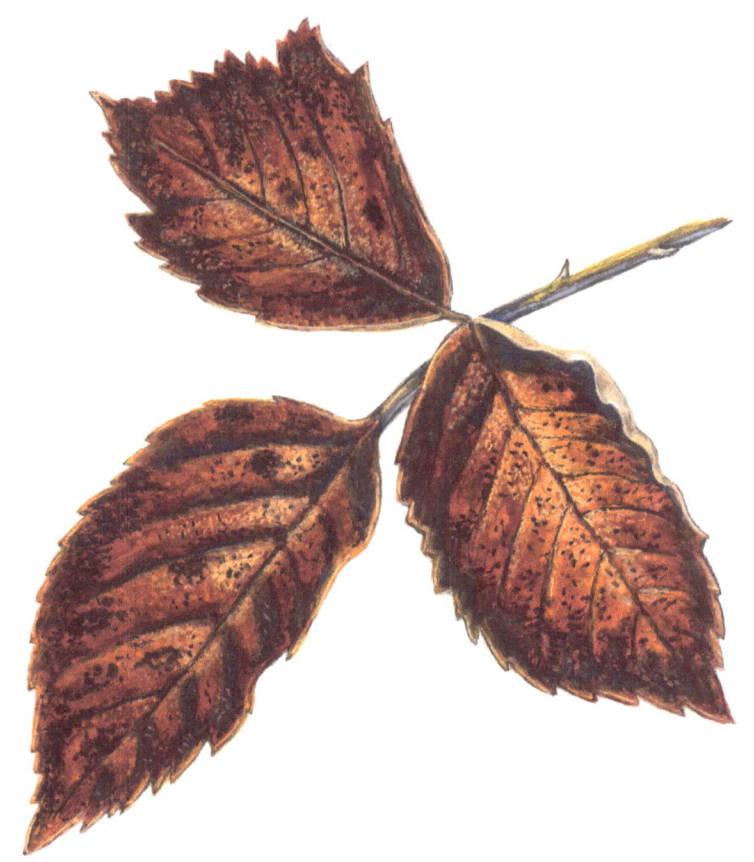

With a slightly damp brush, very gently blend away the sharp edges of the larger dark spots. If you tried to blend the tiny ones they would wash away. With White tinted with a little Ultramarine Blue, paint a line along the lower edge of the stem. Blend it in. This is the reflected light. And, lastly, use a mixture of Burnt Umber and Ultramarine Blue to shade the little part of the leaf that's folded over on the leaf on the bottom right. Make a shadow on the lower side of the undulations of the leaf edge. Blend them in.

Now, stand back and look at your illustration. Run a damp brush around the edges of the leaves to soften them so they don't look pasted on the page. Make adjustments in value. Gouache is easy to change so don't hesitate to rework a portion of the illustration. You may want to put it away for a few days and then reevaluate it before you say "Its done!"

Winter

Winter Weeds
Coneflower, Queen Anne's Lace, Thistle

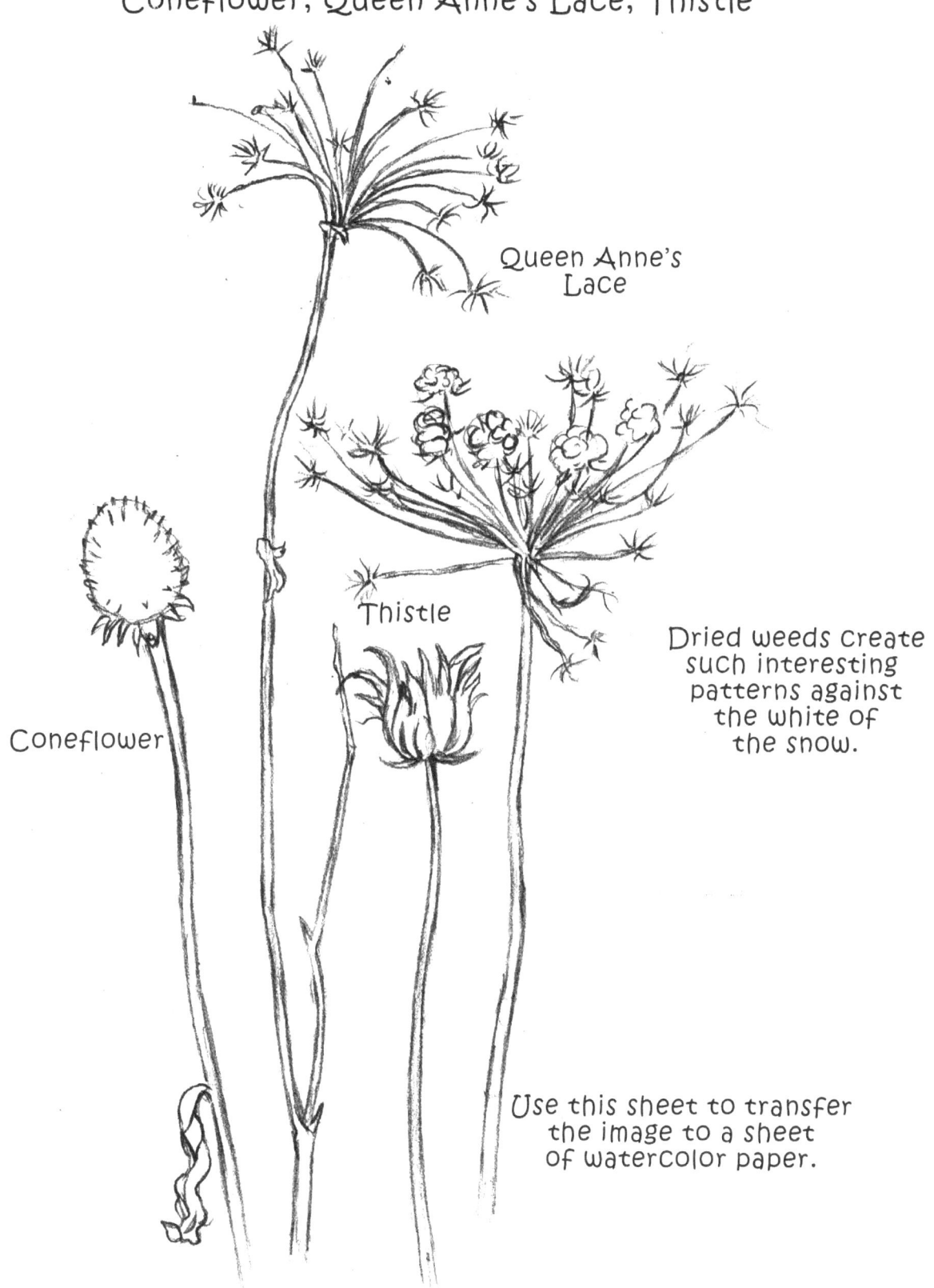

Queen Anne's Lace

Thistle

Coneflower

Dried weeds create such interesting patterns against the white of the snow.

Use this sheet to transfer the image to a sheet of watercolor paper.

Winter Weeds

Colors Used: Yellow Ochre, Permanent White, Ultramarine Blue,
Burnt Umber

(1)

After you transfer the
drawing of the weeds to
your watercolor paper, make
sure your lines are dark
enough so they'll still show
when you begin layering
on gouache. If they're not,
go over them with a very
thin line of Burnt Umber.

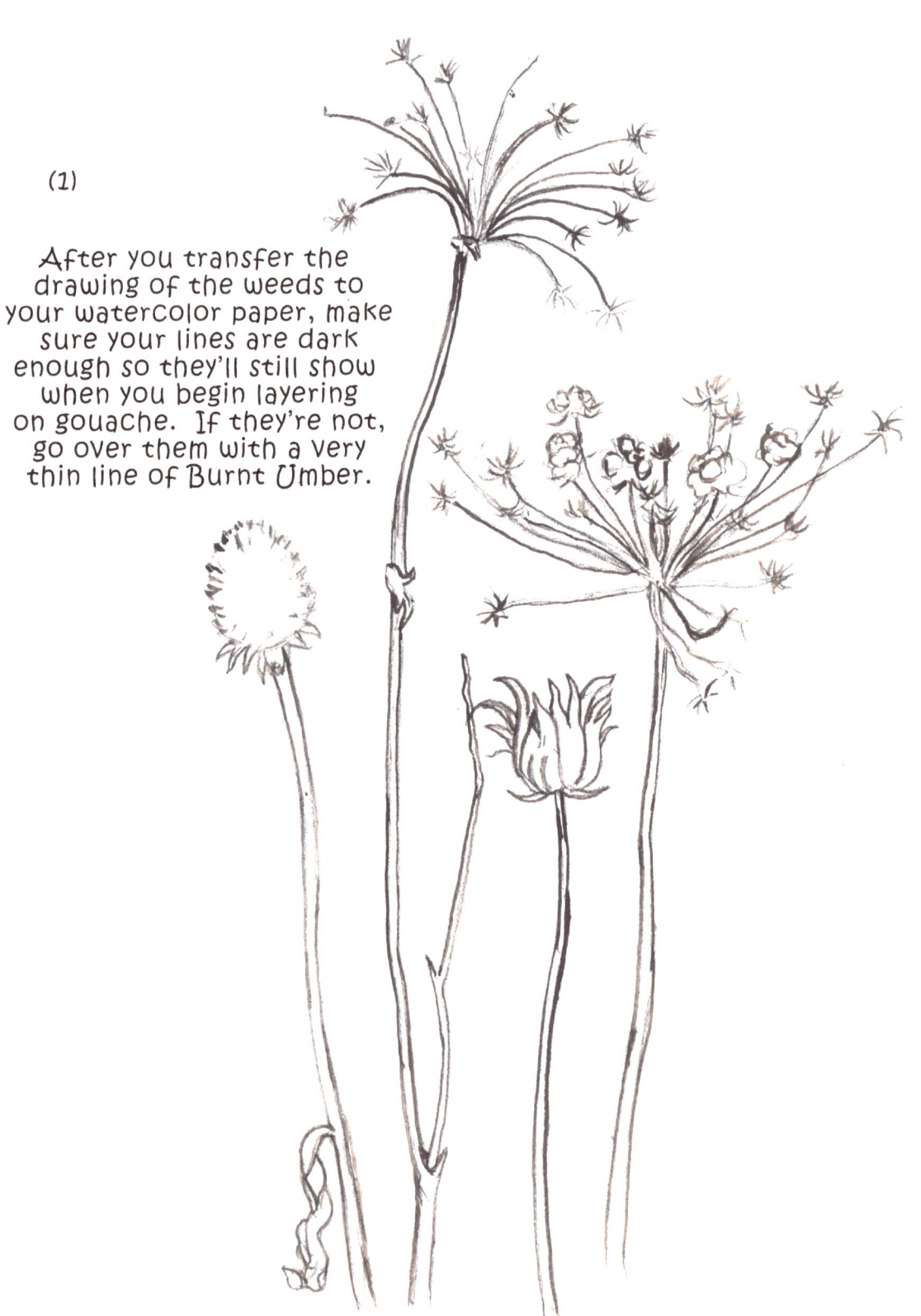

Winter Weeds

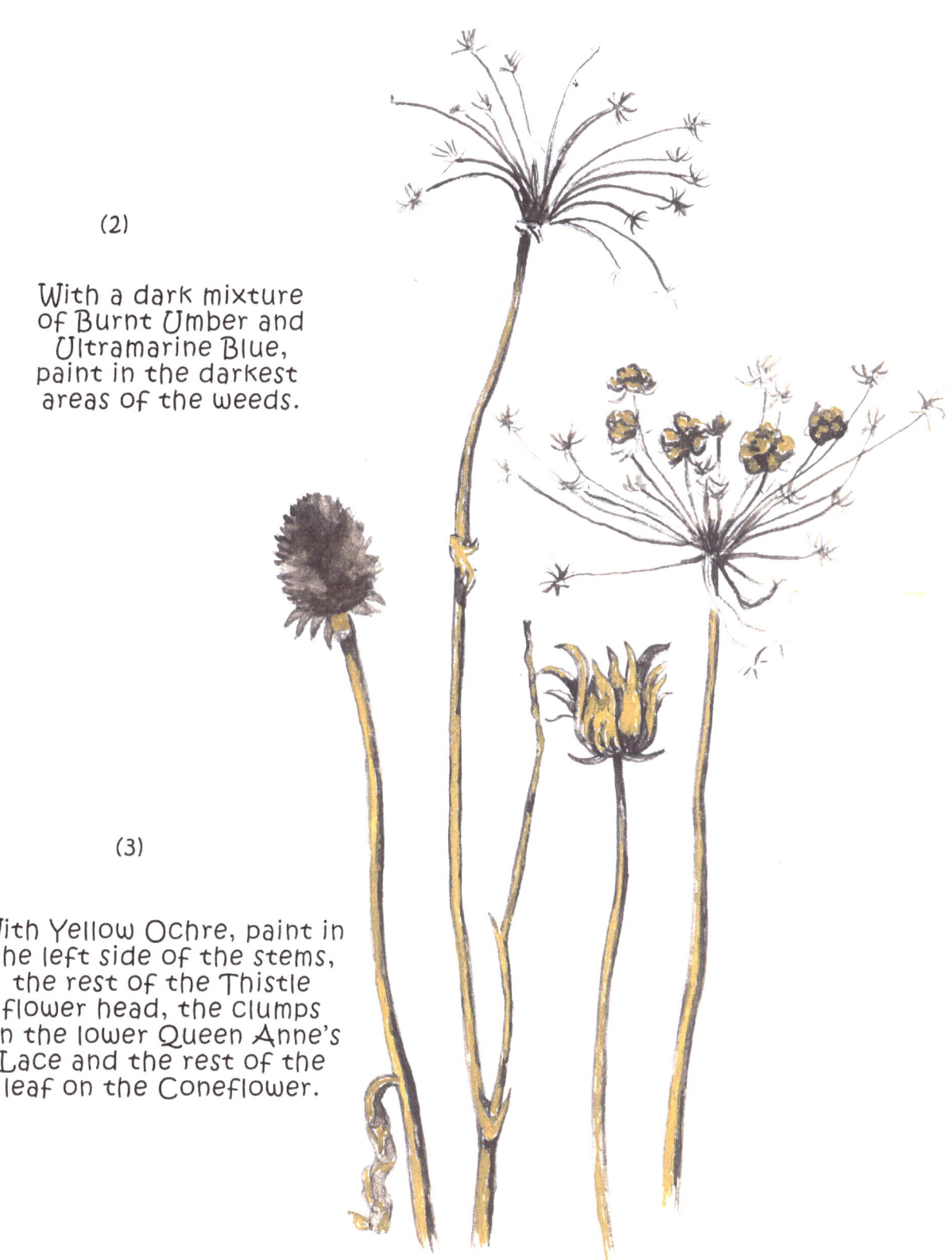

(2)

With a dark mixture
of Burnt Umber and
Ultramarine Blue,
paint in the darkest
areas of the weeds.

(3)

With Yellow Ochre, paint in
the left side of the stems,
the rest of the Thistle
flower head, the clumps
on the lower Queen Anne's
Lace and the rest of the
leaf on the Coneflower.

Winter Weeds

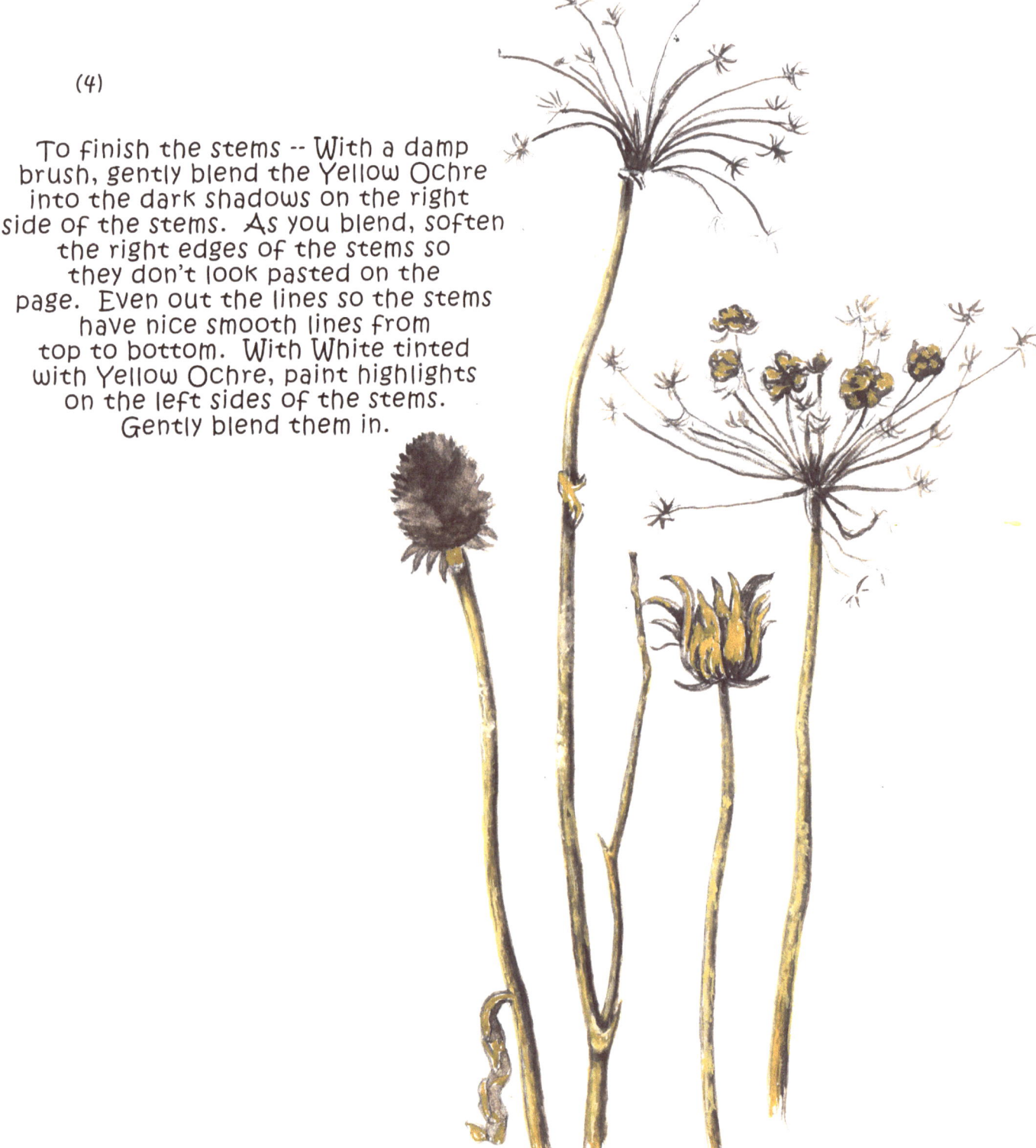

(4)

To finish the stems -- With a damp
brush, gently blend the Yellow Ochre
into the dark shadows on the right
side of the stems. As you blend, soften
the right edges of the stems so
they don't look pasted on the
page. Even out the lines so the stems
have nice smooth lines from
top to bottom. With White tinted
with Yellow Ochre, paint highlights
on the left sides of the stems.
Gently blend them in.

Winter Weeds

(5)

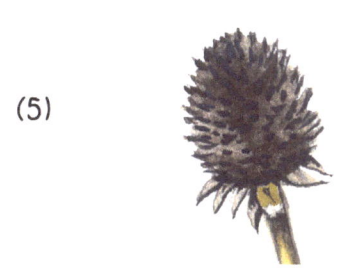

CONEFLOWER HEAD -- With the darkest mixture of Burnt Umber and Ultramarine Blue, paint lines on the lower edges of the tiny, dry leaves encircling the coneflower head. Look carefully at the head and note the direction of each little "spike." Paint lines in the direction of those spikes.

(6)

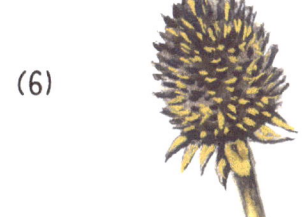

With Yellow Ochre, paint the parts of the tiny leaves that aren't in shadow. Paint this medium value on the little spikes on the flower head. Observe very carefully the size and direction of the spikes. Some will be no more than little dots because of the angle.

(7)

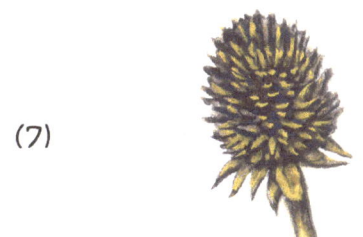

With a very slightly damp, tiny brush, blend the end of each little spike on the end that comes out of the flower head. Leave the forward ends untouched for now. Also, blend the Yellow Ochre into the dark value on the little leaves surrounding the head.

(8)

With White tinted with a little of the Burnt Umber and Ultramarine Blue mixture to make a very light gray, paint the tips of the tiny spikes to highlight them. Also, paint highlights on the dried leaves. With a damp brush, very gently blend off the hard edges of the light value, keeping the very tips of the spikes the lightest value so they appear to come forward.

Winter Weeds

(9)

(10)

Dried Leaf on Coneflower -- With your darkest mixture of Burnt Umber and Ultramarine Blue, paint in the shadow areas of the dried leaf.

With White, paint in the highlighted areas and then, with a damp brush, gently blend the light areas into the dark ones, making smooth transitions between them. Remember to soften the outside edges of the leaf by running a damp brush over them to blur them a little.

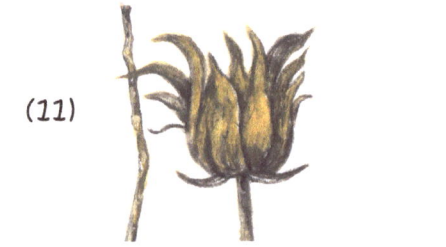

(11)

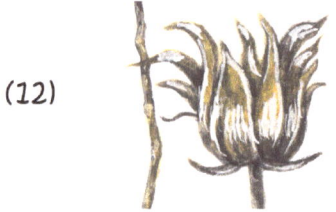

(12)

THISTLE HEAD -- With a slightly damp brush gently blend the medium values into the dark ones you painted previously. Make smooth transitions. Also, soften the outside edges.

With Pure White, paint in the highlights on the thistle head.

Winter Weeds

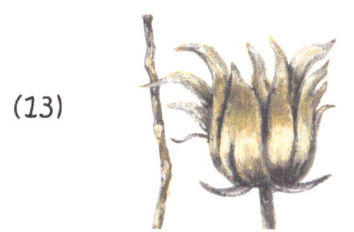

(13)

With a slightly damp brush, blend the highlights into the lower layer of paint. You may have to add more White and blend again as the lower layer of Yellow Ochre mixes with it. You want it to end up a very light ochre, not plain white. You also may have to add a little Burnt Umber toward the top of the leaves and blend it in to get a little shading.

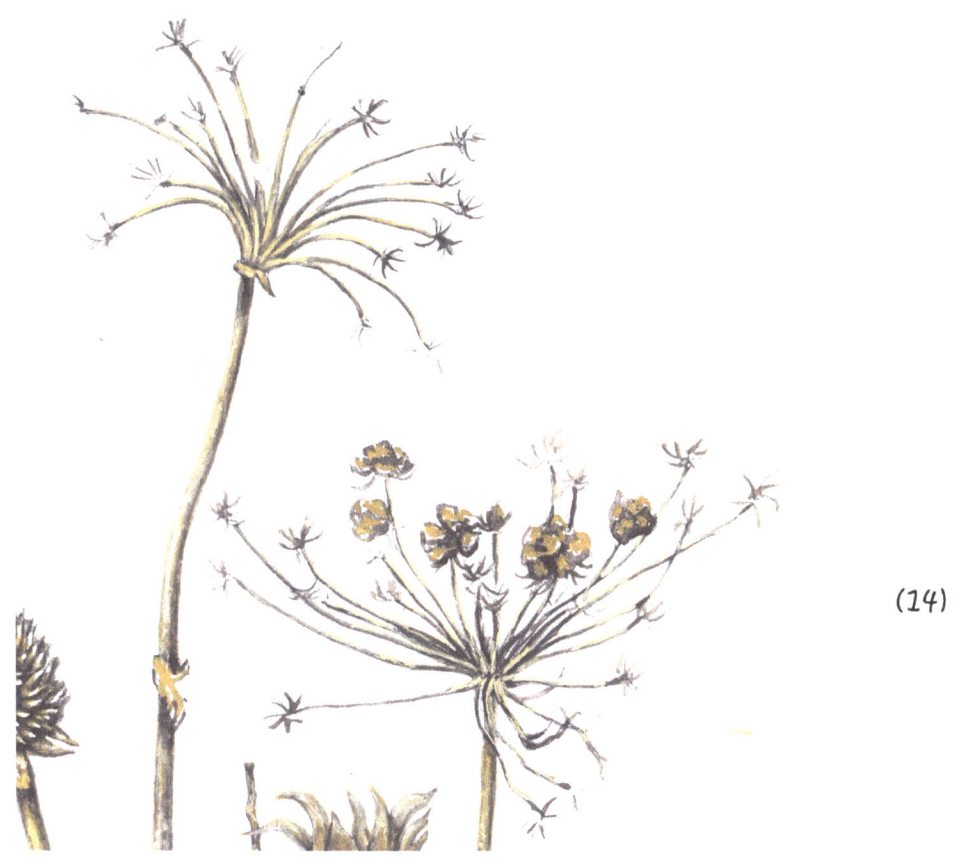

(14)

QUEEN ANNE'S LACE HEADS -- With your finest brush, use Yellow Ochre mixed with White to paint the upper edges of the long branchlettes that you've already painted with Burnt Umber. Very gently blend the colors together. If you lose too much of the light or dark value add more and reblend. Also, blend the outside edges of the lines to soften them so they don't look pasted on the page.

Winter Weeds

(15)

To paint the seed clumps on the head of the Queen Anne's Lace on the right, first gently blend the dark values with the Yellow Ochre that you painted previously.

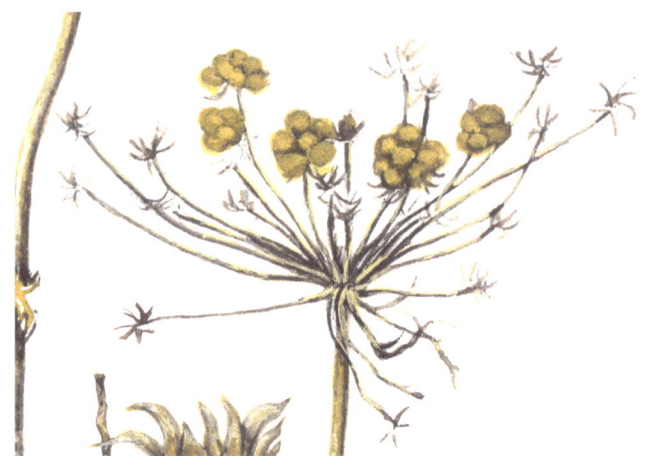

(16)

Detail the seed heads with a dark mixture of Burnt Umber and Ultramarine Blue. To make the narrow pointed lines surrounding the head start your strokes toward the center and lift your brush as you paint outward, making a fine point. With a damp brush, gently soften the edges.

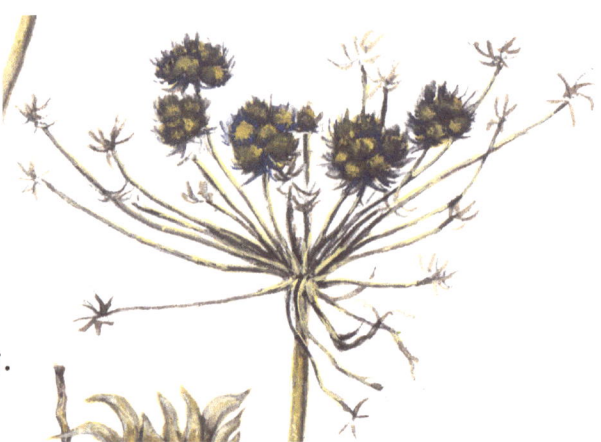

(17)

With White tinted with Yellow Ochre, stipple tiny dots on each segment of the lower Queen Anne's Lace head.

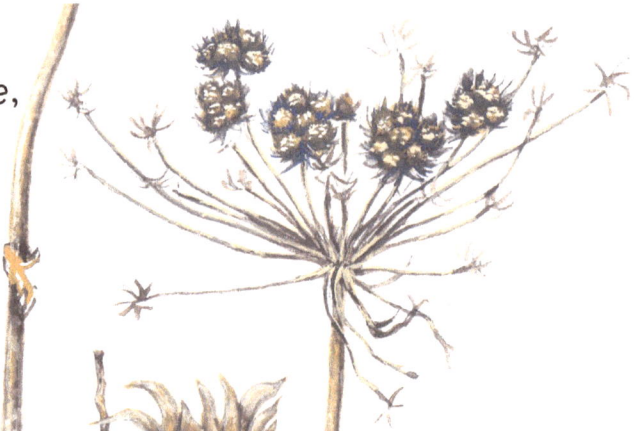

(18)

Gently blend in the White and Yellow Ochre mixture. To finish these little seed heads, use Burnt Umber mixed with Ultramarine Blue to paint some tiny dots on top of the clumps.

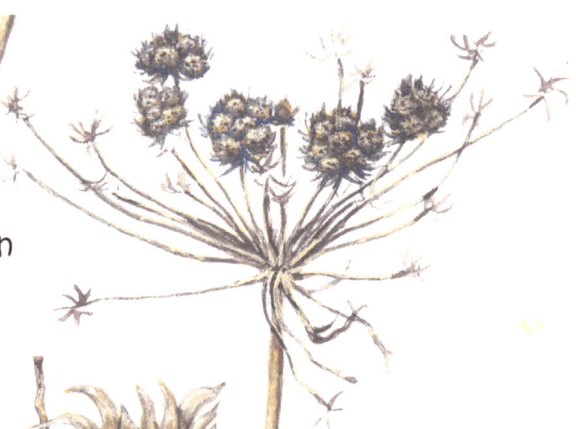

Winter Weeds

(19)

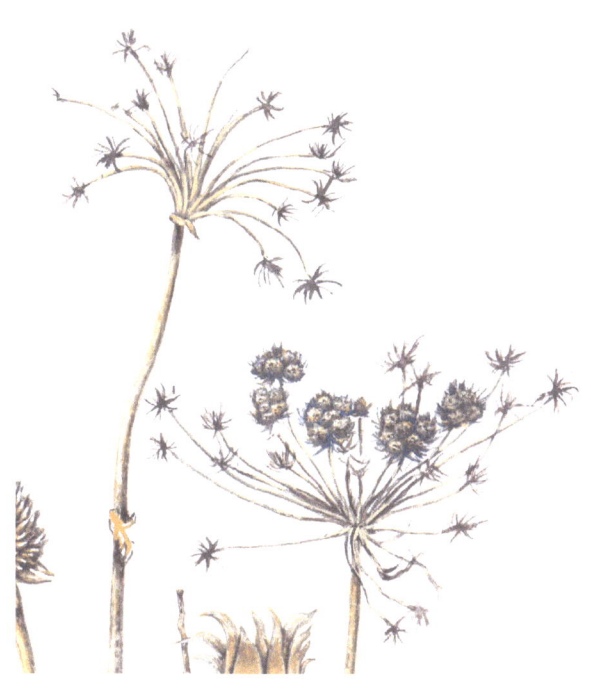

To make the little "stars" on
the ends of the dried branchlettes--
Use Burnt Umber to make a tiny dot
in the center of the stars. Then,
make a quick, short stroke
originating at the the little
dot and going outward, lifting
the brush as you come to the
end of the stroke to make a
fine point. Make sure your
lines are very thin. Don't
make them too regular or
they won't look natural.

(20)

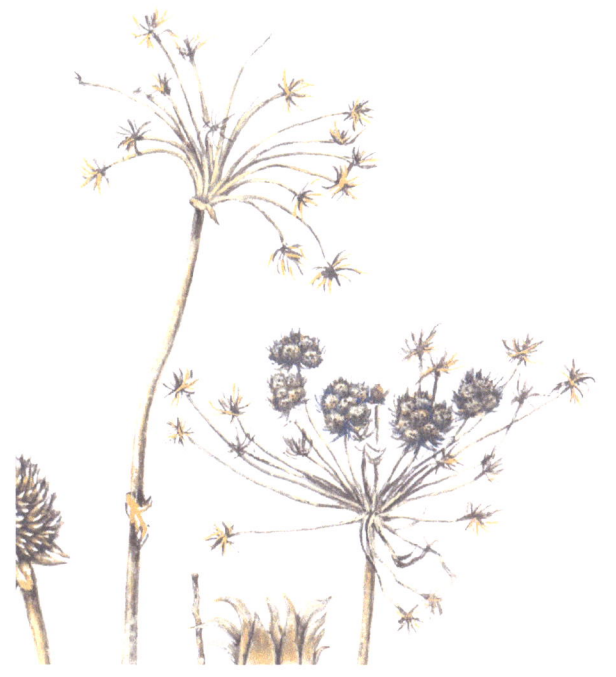

Last step -- With Yellow Ochre,
again make tiny curved strokes
going from the center of the star
outward, lifting your brush
at the end of the stroke to
make tiny points.

Winter Weeds

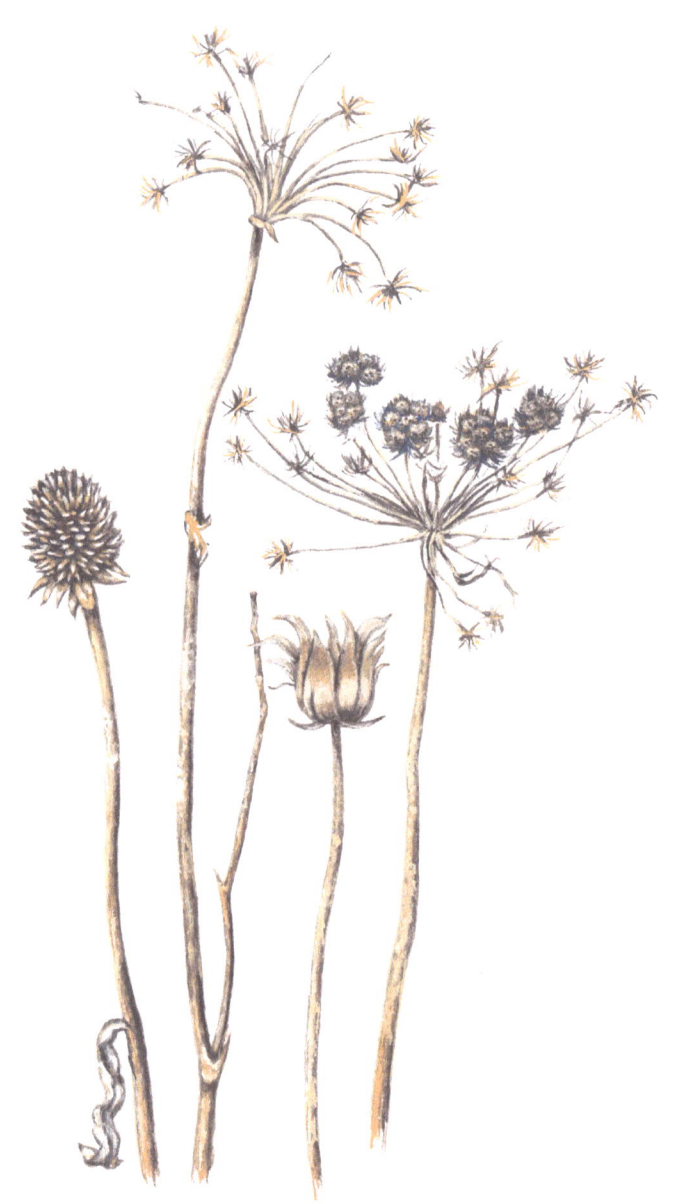

Its always a good idea to stand back, reevaluate
your painting. Make any needed adjustments
in value. Put your illustration aside for a
few days or longer and come back to it with fresh
eyes before you decide "you're done!"

Wrapping Things Up!

The same techniques you've learned to paint seasonal botanicals
in gouache can be used to paint so many of
the creatures and flowers we find around us.
Experiment and find out exactly what works
for you and what subjects most inspire you.

Most of all -- keep painting!

Please check back at
Sound of Wings Studio,
www.soundofwings.com,
for upcoming courses in
painting in gouache.

Thanks!

Sandy

Sandy

Other courses that are currently available are:
   Botanical Illustration in Gouache
   Painting Birds in Gouache
   Painting Animals in Gouache
   Painting Toads and Turtles in Gouache
   Painting Butterflies and Moths in Gouache

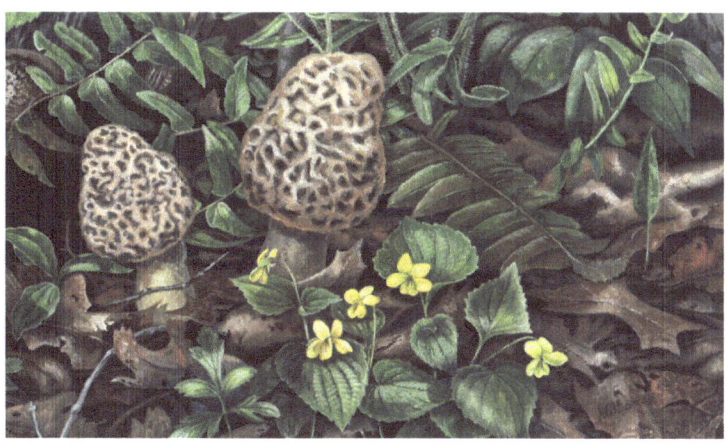